EVERYTHING
AND NOTHING

THE NEW DIRECTIONS *Bibelots*

JORGE LUIS BORGES

EVERYTHING AND NOTHING

TRANSLATED BY DONALD A. YATES, JAMES E. IRBY,
JOHN M. FEIN, AND ELIOT WEINBERGER

Introduction by Donald A. Yates

A NEW DIRECTIONS

D. R. © 1980 by Fondo de Cultura Economica
Copyright © 1984 by Eliot Weinberger
Copyright © 1962, 1964, 1999 by New Directions Publishing
    Corporation
Introduction copyright © 1999 by Donald A. Yates

Manufactured in the United States of America
New Directions Books are printed on acid-free paper.
Published simultaneously in Canada by Penguin Books Canada
    Limited

All writings herein appeared previously in *Labyrinths* and *Seven
Nights,* by Jorge Luis Borges, published 1964 and 1988 respectively
by New Directions. *Everything and Nothing* first published 1999 as a
New Directions Bibelot

Library of Congress Cataloging-in-Publication Data
Borges, Jorge Luis, 1899–
    Everything and nothing / Jorge Luis Borges ; translated by Donald
  A. Yates . . . [et al.] ; introduction by Donald A. Yates.
        p.   cm.
    Contents: Nightmares—Blindness—Tlön, Uqbar, Orbis Tertius—
The garden of forking paths—Death and the compass—The wall and
the books—Kafka and his precursors—Everything & nothing—
Borges and I.
    ISBN-13: 978-0-8112-1400-1 / ISBN-10: 0-8112-1400-1
    1. Borges, Jorge Luis, 1899–   —Translations into English.
I. Title.   II. Title: Everything and nothing.
PQ7797.B635A6   1999
868—dc21   98-54217
                                                                        CIP

New Directions Books are published for James Laughlin
by New Directions Publishing Corporation
80 Eighth Avenue, New York 10011

FIFTH PRINTING

Table of Contents

Introduction

When the first English-language collections of the writings of Jorge Luis Borges appeared in 1962, they attracted immediate critical attention. But almost as remarkable as the singular flavor of these story-like essays and essay-like fictions was the knowledge that Borges, virtually unknown in the U.S. until then, had been elaborating these strikingly original narratives in the distant confines of his native Argentina. That this author quietly, almost secretly, had been producing in Buenos Aires, so far removed from the crossroads of western culture, a body of work that unquestionably placed him among the major writers of our time was a part of the mystique that came to surround the blind poet and his work.

He was born a century ago on August 24, 1899, in Buenos Aires, spent the years from 1914 to 1921 with his family in Switzerland and in Spain, and after the early twenties rarely ever left his homeland. Nonetheless he had taken from his years in Europe and from his English-speaking father—a widely-read teacher of psychology—a broad experience of literature. He spoke Spanish, English, French, and German and read Italian and Latin.

During his early years he was a poet and author of critical essays dealing with literary and philosophical topics. He did not attempt to write fiction since it was his firm belief that the accomplishments of the prose writers he most admired—particularly Stevenson, Chesterton, and Kipling—were far beyond his own abilities. Yet, in the end, it was a writer of short stories that he became most noted.

Intensely self-critical, he rejected almost everything that he wrote in the twenties, and set out in the thirties to temper his elegant but compulsively innovative and aggressive literary voice. By the end of that decade, he had accumulated enough experience and judgment to consider that he might—tentatively—attempt to write narrative fiction.

The first five stories included here are taken from his 1944 collection of what are commonly designated as his (no other term seems suitable) "ficciones." It is astonishing to realize that these masterful stories are among his first creations as an author of narrative prose.

"Pierre Menard, Author of the *Quixote*" was Borges's first deliberate try at writing his own kind of short story. In a real sense, it quite subtly anticipated critical literary theory that would emerge a quarter of a century later. "Tlön, Uqbar, Orbis Tertius" is an extraordinarily ambitious story, considering that it was only the second "ficción" that Borges wrote. In the space of some fifteen pages, the reader is witness to nothing less than the phenomenon of our own world being taken over by another one, constructed on philosophical and metaphysical speculations. In "The Lottery in Babylon," with humor and precision, Borges sketches out a metaphor of human existence. Clearly, when he overcame his own reluctance and began writing stories, no subject was too recondite to be dealt with in fictional terms.

The last two of these early tales—all written between 1939 and 1942—are among the most memorable and most accessible of Borges's stories. Here he takes two popular narrative forms—the espionage story and the detective story—and infuses them with his characteristically disconcerting intellectual tone. Dr. Yu Tsun and Stephen Albert in "The Garden of Forking Paths" and Erik Lönnrot and Red Scharlach in "Death and the Compass" are something other than flesh-and-blood characters. In Borges's hands, they serve to give unaccustomed dramatic expression to certain philosophical concepts.

The short essays that follow, "The Wall and the Books" and "Kafka and His Precursors," appeared in Borges's last collection of essays, *Otras inquisiciones,* published in Buenos Aires in 1952 and in English translation as *Other Inquisitions* in 1964. The sense of inconclusiveness and uncertainty in the first of these is a mood typically encountered in Borges's essays, where intellectual speculation is everything and conclusive truth inevitably eludes the author's grasp. The Kafka piece is one of many of Borges's essays in which he offers the reader the results of incessant examination of the essentials of the literary experience. The idea that, in a way, a writer can *create* his own precursors is startling, but Borges's reasoned argument is seductive.

In 1955 Borges lost his sight for the purpose of reading and writing, and thereafter considered that he would be able to write only short prose pieces. The laborious correcting and revising of his manuscript pages was a thing of the past. Yet he was still able to compose in his head and thus fashion short parables that he would mentally revise until they were ready to be committed to paper. In February of 1957, Borges dictated to his mother, Leonor Acevedo de Borges, his hauntingly ambiguous "Borges and I." It is surely one of the most perfectly poised pages in the literature of this century and one that gives an insight into Borges's view of himself as a man and as a literary personality. The last prose sketch included here is "Everything and Nothing," which stands as a kind of confessional look back over his long career as a creative artist.

Doubt, weariness, and anxiety are combined in this brief evocation of a vision that is peculiarly Borges's own.

After he lost his sight, Borges turned increasingly to the public lecture as a medium in which to communicate his unique understanding of the many things he had read and experienced in his lifetime. "Nightmares" and "Blindness" are the transcriptions of two lectures he gave in Buenos Aires in mid-1977. He had always been able to call upon long-remembered passages from works that he had read—poetry as well as prose, in half a dozen languages—and it was those that he was able to weave into the contexts of his informal lectures. In these two talks, similar to those he gave over the period of three decades and in many parts of the world to which, now famous and much honored, he had been invited, he offers generous glimpses into his personal perplexities and intellectual concerns.

When he died on June 14, 1986, in Geneva, Switzerland, one thing was abundantly clear. The world could never hope to see another Borges.

Donald A. Yates

EVERYTHING AND NOTHING

Pierre Menard,
Author of the *Quixote*

The *visible* work left by this novelist is easily and briefly enumerated. Impardonable, therefore, are the omissions and additions perpetrated by Madame Henri Bachelier in a fallacious catalogue which a certain daily, whose *Protestant* tendency is no secret, has had the inconsideration to inflict upon its deplorable readers—though these be few and Calvinist, if not Masonic and circumcised. The true friends of Menard have viewed this catalogue with alarm and even with a certain melancholy. One might say that only yesterday we gathered before his final monument, amidst the lugubrious cypresses, and already Error tries to tarnish his Memory . . . Decidedly, a brief rectification is unavoidable.

I am aware that it is quite easy to challenge my slight authority. I hope, however, that I shall not be prohibited from mentioning two eminent testimonies. The Baroness de Bacourt (at whose unforgettable *vendredis* I had the honor of meeting the lamented poet) has seen fit to approve the pages which follow. The Countess de Bagnoregio, one of the most delicate spirits of the Principality of Monaco (and now of Pittsburgh, Pennsylvania, following her recent marriage to the international philanthropist Simon Kautzsch, who has been so inconsiderately slandered, alas! by the victims of his disinterested maneuvers) has sacrificed "to veracity and to death" (such were her words) the stately reserve which is her distinction, and, in an open letter published in the magazine *Luxe,* concedes me her approval as well. These authorizations, I think, are not entirely insufficient.

I have said that Menard's visible work can be easily enumerated. Having examined with care his personal files, I find that they contain the following items:

a) A Symbolist sonnet which appeared twice (with variants) in the review *La conque* (issues of March and October 1899).

b) A monograph on the possibility of constructing a poetic vocabulary of concepts which would not be synonyms or periphrases of those which make up our everyday language, "but rather ideal objects created according to convention and essentially designed to satisfy poetic needs" (Nîmes, 1901).

c) A monograph on "certain connections or affinities" between the thought of Descartes, Leibniz and John Wilkins (Nîmes, 1903).

d) A monograph on Leibniz's *Characteristica universalis* (Nîmes, 1904).

e) A technical article on the possibility of improving the game of chess, eliminating one of the rook's pawns. Menard proposes, recommends, discusses and finally rejects this innovation.

f) A monograph on Raymond Lully's *Ars magna generalis* (Nîmes, 1906).

g) A translation, with prologue and notes, of Ruy López de Segura's *Libro de la invención liberal y arte del juego del axedrez* (Paris, 1907).

h) The work sheets of a monograph on George Boole's symbolic logic.

i) An examination of the essential metric laws of French prose, illustrated with examples taken from Saint-Simon (*Revue des langues romanes,* Montpellier, October 1909).

j) A reply to Luc Durtain (who had denied the existence of such laws), illustrated with examples from Luc Durtain (*Revue des langues romanes,* Montpellier, December 1909).

k) A manuscript translation of the *Aguja de navegar cultos* of Quevedo, entitled *La boussole des précieux.*

l) A preface to the Catalogue of an exposition of lithographs by Carolus Hourcade (Nîmes, 1914).

m) The work *Les problèmes d'un problème* (Paris, 1917), which discusses, in chronological order, the different solutions given to the illustrous problem of Achilles and the tortoise. Two editions of this book have appeared so far; the second bears as an epigraph Leibniz's recommendation *"Ne craignez point, monsieur, la tortue"* and revises the chapters dedicated to Russell and Descartes.

n) A determined analysis of the "syntactical customs" of Toulet (*N. R. F.,* March 1921). Menard—I recall—declared that censure and praise are sentimental operations which have nothing to do with literary criticism.

o) A transposition into alexandrines of Paul Valéry's *Le cimetière marin* (*N. R. F.,* January 1928).

p) An invective against Paul Valéry, in the *Papers for the Suppression of Reality* of Jacques Reboul. (This invective, we might say parenthetically, is the exact opposite of his true opinion of Valéry. The latter understood it as such and their old friendship was not endangered.)

q) A "definition" of the Countess de Bagnoregio, in the "victorious volume"—the locution is Gabriele d'Annunzio's, another of its collaborators—published annually by this lady to rectify the inevitable falsifications of journalists and to present "to the world and to Italy" an authentic image of her person, so often exposed (by very reason of her beauty and her activities) to erroneous or hasty interpretations.

r) A cycle of admirable sonnets for the Baroness de Bacourt (1934).

s) A manuscript list of verses which owe their efficacy to their punctuation.[1]

This, then, is the *visible* work of Menard, in chronological order (with no omission other than a few vague sonnets of circumstance written for the hospitable, or avid, album of Madame Henri Bachelier). I turn now to his other work: the subterranean, the interminably heroic, the peerless. And—such are the capacities of man!—the unfinished. This work, perhaps the most significant of our time, consists of the ninth and thirty-eighth chapters of the first part of *Don Quixote* and a fragment of chapter twenty-two. I know such an affirmation seems an absurdity; to justify this "absurdity" is the primordial object of this note.[2]

Two texts of unequal value inspired this undertaking. One is that philological fragment by Novalis—the one numbered 2005 in the Dresden edition—which outlines the theme of a *total* identification with a given author. The other is one of those parasitic books which situate Christ on a boulevard, Hamlet on La Cannebière or Don Quixote on Wall Street.

[1]Madame Henri Bachelier also lists a literal translation of Quevedo's literal translation of the *Introduction à la vie dévote* of St. Francis of Sales. There are no traces of such a work in Menard's library. It must have been a jest of our friend, misunderstood by the lady.

[2]I also had the secondary intention of sketching a personal portrait of Pierre Menard. But how could I dare to compete with the golden pages which, I am told, the Baroness de Bacourt is preparing or with the delicate and punctual pencil of Carolus Hourcade?

4

Like all men of good taste, Menard abhorred these useless carnivals, fit only—as he would say—to produce the plebeian pleasure of anachronism or (what is worse) to enthrall us with the elementary idea that all epochs are the same or are different. More interesting, though contradictory and superficial of execution, seemed to him the famous plan of Daudet: to conjoin the Ingenious Gentleman and his squire in *one* figure, which was Tartarin . . . Those who have insinuated that Menard dedicated his life to writing a contemporary *Quixote* calumniate his illustrious memory.

He did not want to compose another *Quixote*—which is easy—but *the Quixote itself.* Needless to say, he never contemplated a mechanical transcription of the original; he did not propose to copy it. His admirable intention was to produce a few pages which would coincide—word for word and line for line—with those of Miguel Cervantes.

"My intent is no more than astonishing," he wrote me the 30th of September, 1934, from Bayonne. "The final term in a theological or metaphysical demonstration—the objective world, God, causality, the forms of the universe—is no less previous and common than my famed novel. The only difference is that the philosophers publish the intermediary stages of their labor in pleasant volumes and I have resolved to do away with those stages." In truth, not one worksheet remains to bear witness to his years of effort.

The first method he conceived was relatively simple. Know Spanish well, recover the Catholic faith, fight against the Moors or the Turk, forget the history of Europe between the years 1602 and 1918, *be* Miguel de Cervantes. Pierre Menard studied this procedure (I know he attained a fairly accurate command of seventeenth-century Spanish) but discarded it as too easy. Rather as impossible! my reader will say. Granted, but the undertaking was impossible from the very beginning

5

and of all the impossible ways of carrying it out, this was the least interesting. To be, in the twentieth century, a popular novelist of the seventeenth seemed to him a diminution. To be, in some way, Certvantes and reach the *Quixote* seemed less arduous to him—and, consequently, less interesting—than to go on being Pierre Menard and reach the *Quixote* through the experiences of Pierre Menard. (This conviction, we might say in passing, made him omit the autobiographical prologue to the second part of *Don Quixote*. To include that prologue would have been to create another character—Cervantes— but it would also have meant presenting the *Quixote* in terms of that character and not of Menard. The latter, naturally, de- clined that facility.) "My undertaking is not difficult, essen- tially," I read in another part of his letter. "I should only have to be immortal to carry it out." Shall I confess that I often imagine he did finish it and that I read the *Quixote*—all of it— as if Menard had conceived it? Some nights past, while leafing through chapter XXVI—never essayed by him—I recognized our friend's style and something of his voice in this exceptional phrase: "the river nymphs and the dolorous and humid Echo." This happy conjunction of a spiritual and a physical adjective brought to my mind a verse by Shakespeare which we dis- cussed one afternoon:

> Where a malignant and a turbaned Turk . . .

But why precisely the *Quixote*? our reader will ask. Such a preference, in a Spaniard, would not have been inexplicable; but it is, no doubt, in a Symbolist from Nîmes, essentially a de- voté of Poe, who engendered Baudelaire, who engendered Mallarmé, who engendered Valéry, who engendered Edmond Teste. The aforementioned letter illuminates this point. "The *Quixote*," clarifies Menard, "interests me deeply, but it does

6

not seem—how shall I say it?—inevitable. I cannot imagine the universe without Edgar Allan Poe's exclamation:

Ah, bear in mind this garden was enchanted!

or without the *Bateau ivre* or the *Ancient Mariner,* but I am quite capable of imagining it without the *Quixote.* (I speak, naturally, of my personal capacity and not of those works' historical resonance.) The *Quixote* is a contingent book; the *Quixote* is unnecessary. I can premeditate writing it, I can write it, without falling into a tautology. When I was ten or twelve years old, I read it, perhaps in its entirety. Later, I have reread closely certain chapters, those which I shall not attempt for the time being. I have also gone through the interludes, the plays, the *Galatea,* the exemplary novels, the undoubtedly laborious tribulations of Persiles and Segismunda and the *Viaje del Parnaso* . . . My general recollection of the *Quixote,* simplified by forgetfulness and indifference, can well equal the imprecise and prior image of a book not yet written. Once that image (which no one can legitimately deny me) is postulated, it is certain that my problem is a good bit more difficult than Cervantes' was. My obliging predecessor did not refuse the collaboration of chance: he composed his immortal work somewhat *à la diable,* carried along by the inertias of language and invention. I have taken on the mysterious duty of reconstructing literally his spontaneous work. My solitary game is governed by two polar laws. The first permits me to essay variations of a formal or psychological type; the second obliges me to sacrifice these variations to the "original" text and reason out this annihilation in an irrefutable manner . . . To these artificial hindrances, another—of a congenital kind— must be added. To compose the *Quixote* at the beginning of the seventeenth century was a reasonable undertaking, neces-

7

sary and perhaps even unavoidable; at the beginning of the twentieth, it is almost impossible. It is not in vain that three hundred years have gone by, filled with exceedingly complex events. Amongst them, to mention only one, is the *Quixote* itself."

In spite of these three obstacles, Menard's fragmentary *Quixote* is more subtle than Cervantes'. The latter, in a clumsy fashion, opposes to the fictions of chivalry the tawdry provincial reality of his country; Menard selects as his "reality" the land of Carmen during the century of Lepanto and Lope de Vega. What a series of *espagnolades* that selection would have suggested to Maurice Barrès or Dr. Rodríguez Larreta! Menard eludes them with complete naturalness. In his work there are no gypsy flourishes or conquistadors or mystics or Philip the Seconds or *autos da fé*. He neglects or eliminates local color. This disdain points to a new conception of the historical novel. This disdain condemns *Salammbô*, with no possibility of appeal.

It is no less astounding to consider isolated chapters. For example, let us examine Chapter XXXVIII of the first part, "which treats of the curious discourse of Don Quixote on arms and letters." It is well known that Don Quixote (like Quevedo in an analogous and later passage in *La hora de todos*) decided the debate against letters and in favor of arms. Cervantes was a former soldier: his verdict is understandable. But that Pierre Menard's Don Quixote—a contemporary of *La trahison des clercs* and Bertrand Russell—should fall prey to such nebulous sophistries! Madame Bachelier has seen here an admirable and typical subordination on the part of the author to the hero's psychology; others (not at all perspicaciously), a *transcription* of the *Quixote;* the Baroness de Bacourt, the influence of Nietzsche. To this third interpretation (which I judge to be irrefutable) I am not sure I dare to add a fourth, which concords very well with the almost divine modesty of Pierre Menard: his resigned or ironical habit of propagating ideas which were the strict reverse of those he preferred. (Let us recall once more his diatribe against Paul Valéry in Jacques Reboul's ephemeral Surrealist sheet.) Cervantes' text and Menard's are verbally identical, but the second is almost infinitely richer. (More ambiguous, his detractors will say, but ambiguity is richness.)

It is a revelation to compare Menard's *Don Quixote* with Cervantes'. The latter, for example, wrote (part one, chapter nine):

. . . truth, whose mother is history, rival of time, depository of deeds, witness of the past, exemplar and adviser to the present, and the future's counselor.

Written in the seventeenth century, written by the "lay genius" Cervantes, this enumeration is a mere rhetorical praise of history. Menard, on the other hand, writes:

. . . truth, whose mother is history, rival of time, depository of deeds, witness of the past, exemplar and adviser to the present, and the future's counselor.

History, the *mother* of truth: the idea is astounding. Menard, a contemporary of William James, does not define history as an inquiry into reality but as its origin. Historical truth, for him, is not what has happened; it is what we judge to have happened. The final phrases—*exemplar and adviser to the present, and the future's counselor*—are brazenly pragmatic.

The contrast in style is also vivid. The archaic style of Menard—quite foreign, after all—suffers from a certain affectation. Not so that of his forerunner, who handles with ease the current Spanish of his time.

9

There is no exercise of the intellect which is not, in the final analysis, useless. A philosophical doctrine begins as a plausible description of the universe; with the passage of the years it becomes a mere chapter—if not a paragraph or a name—in the history of philosophy. In literature, this eventual caducity is even more notorious. The *Quixote*—Menard told me—was, above all, an entertaining book; now it is the occasion for patriotic toasts, grammatical insolence and obscene de luxe editions. Fame is a form of incomprehension, perhaps the worst.

There is nothing new in these nihilistic verifications; what is singular is the determination Menard derived from them. He decided to anticipate the vanity awaiting all man's efforts; he set himself to an undertaking which was exceedingly complex and, from the very beginning, futile. He dedicated his scruples and his sleepless nights to repeating an already extant book in an alien tongue. He multiplied draft upon draft, revised tenaciously and tore up thousands of manuscript pages.[1] He did not let anyone examine these drafts and took care they should not survive him. In vain have I tried to reconstruct them.

I have reflected that it is permissible to see in this "final" *Quixote* a kind of palimpsest, through which the traces—tenuous but not indecipherable—of our friend's "previous" writing should be translucently visible. Unfortunately, only a second Pierre Menard, inverting the other's work, would be able to exhume and revive those lost Troys . . .

"Thinking, analyzing, inventing (he also wrote me) are not

[1] I remember his quadricular notebooks, his black crossed-out passages, his peculiar typographical symbols and his insect-like handwriting. In the afternoons he liked to go out for a walk around the outskirts of Nîmes; he would take a notebook with him and make a merry bonfire.

anomalous acts; they are normal respiration of the intelligence. To glorify the occasional performance of that function, to hoard ancient and alien thoughts, to recall with incredulous stupor that the *doctor universalis* thought, is to confess our laziness or our barbarity. Every man should be capable of all ideas and I understand that in the future this will be the case."

Menard (perhaps without wanting to) has enriched, by means of a new technique, the halting and rudimentary art of reading: this new technique is that of the deliberate anachronism and the erroneous attribution. This technique, whose applications are infinite, prompts us to go through the *Odyssey* as if it were posterior to the *Aeneid* and the book *Le jardin du Centaure* of Madame Henri Bachelier as if it were by Madame Henri Bachelier. This technique fills the most placid works with adventure. To attribute the *Imitatio Christi* to Louis Ferdinand Céline or to James Joyce, is this not a sufficient renovation of its tenuous spiritual indications?

For Silvina Ocampo

Translated by James E. Irby

Tlön, Uqbar, Orbis Tertius

I

I owe the discovery of Uqbar to the conjunction of a mirror and an encyclopedia. The mirror troubled the depths of a corridor in a country house on Gaona Street in Ramos Mejía; the encyclopedia is fallaciously called *The Anglo-American Cyclopaedia* (New York, 1917) and is a literal but delinquent reprint of the *Encyclopaedia Britannica* of 1902. The event took place some five years ago. Bioy Casares had had dinner with me that evening and we became lengthily engaged in a vast polemic concerning the composition of a novel in the first person, whose narrator would omit or disfigure the facts and indulge in various contradictions which would permit a few readers—very few readers—to perceive an atrocious or banal reality. From the remote depths of the corridor, the mirror spied upon us. We discovered (such a discovery is inevitable in the late hours of the night) that mirrors have something monstrous about them. Then Bioy Casares recalled that one of the heresiarchs of Uqbar had declared that mirrors and copulation are abominable, because they increase the number of men. I asked him the origin of this memorable observation and he answered that it was reproduced in *The Anglo-American Cyclopaedia*, in its article on Uqbar. The house (which we had rented furnished) had a set of this work. On the last pages of Volume XLVI we

12

found an article on Upsala; on the first pages of Volume XLVII, one on Ural-Altaic Languages, but not a word about Uqbar. Bioy, a bit taken aback, consulted the volumes of the index. In vain he exhausted all of the imaginable spellings: Ukbak, Ucbar, Ooqbar, Oukbahr . . . Before leaving, he told me that it was a region of Iraq or of Asia Minor. I must confess that I agreed with some discomfort. I conjectured that this undocumented country and its anonymous heresiarch were a fiction devised by Bioy's modesty in order to justify a statement. The fruitless examination of one of Justus Perthes' atlases fortified my doubt.

The following day, Bioy called me from Buenos Aires. He told me he had before him the article on Uqbar, in Volume XLVI of the encyclopedia. The heresiarch's name was not forthcoming, but there was a note on his doctrine, formulated in words almost identical to those he had repeated, though perhaps literarily inferior. He had recalled: *Copulation and mirrors are abominable.* The text of the encyclopedia said: *For one of those gnostics, the visible universe was an illusion or (more precisely) a sophism. Mirrors and fatherhood are abominable because they multiply and disseminate that universe.* I told him, in all truthfulness, that I should like to see that article. A few days later he brought it. This suprised me, since the scrupulous cartographical indices of Ritter's *Erdkunde* were plentifully ignorant of the name Uqbar.

The tome Bioy brought was, in fact, Volume XLVI of the *Anglo-American Cyclopaedia.* On the half-title page and the spine, the alphabetical marking (Tor-Ups) was that of our copy, but, instead of 917, it contained 921 pages. These four additional pages made up the article on Uqbar, which (as the reader will have noticed) was not indicated by the alphabetical marking. We later determined that there was no other difference between the volumes. Both of them (as I believe I have

13

indicated) are reprints of the tenth *Encyclopaedia Britannica*. Bioy had acquired his copy at some sale or other.

We read the article with some care. The passage recalled by Bioy was perhaps the only surprising one. The rest of it seemed very plausible, quite in keeping with the general tone of the work and (as is natural) a bit boring. Reading it over again, we discovered beneath its rigorous prose a fundamental vagueness. Of the fourteen names which figured in the geographical part, we only recognized three—Khorasan, Armenia, Erzerum—interpolated in the text in an ambiguous way. Of the historical names, only one: the impostor magician Smerdis, invoked more as a metaphor. The note seemed to fix the boundaries of Uqbar, but its nebulous reference points were rivers and craters and mountain ranges of that same region. We read, for example, that the lowlands of Tsai Khaldun and the Axa Delta marked the southern frontier and that on the islands of the delta wild horses procreate. All this, on the first part of page 918. In the historical section (page 920) we learned that as a result of the religious persecutions of the thirteenth century, the orthodox believers sought refuge on these islands, where to this day their obelisks remain and where it is not uncommon to unearth their stone mirrors. The section on Language and Literature was brief. Only one trait is worthy of recollection: it noted that the literature of Uqbar was one of fantasy and that its epics and legends never referred to reality, but to the two imaginary regions of Mlejnas and Tlön . . . The bibliography enumerated four volumes which we have not yet found, though the third—Silas Haslam: *History of the Land Called Uqbar*, 1874—figures in the catalogues of Bernard Quaritch's book shop.[1] The first, *Lesbare und lesenswerthe Bemerkungen über das Land Ukkbar in*

---

[1]Haslam has also published *A General History of Labyrinths*.

Klein-Asien, dates from 1641 and is the work of Johannes Valentinus Andreä. This fact is significant; a few years later, I came upon that name in the unsuspected pages of De Quincey (*Writings,* Volume XIII) and learned that it belonged to a German theologian who, in the early seventeenth century, described the imaginary community of Rosae Crucis—a community that others founded later, in imitation of what he had prefigured.

That night we visited the National Library. In vain we exhausted atlases, catalogues, annuals of geographical societies, travelers' and historians' memoirs: no one had ever been in Uqbar. Neither did the general index of Bioy's encyclopedia register that name. The following day, Carlos Mastronardi (to whom I had related the matter) noticed the black and gold covers of the *Anglo-American Cyclopaedia* in a bookshop on Corrientes and Talcahuano . . . He entered and examined Volume XLVI. Of course, he did not find the slightest indication of Uqbar.

II

Some limited and waning memory of Herbert Ashe, an engineer of the southern railways, persists in the hotel at Adrogué, amongst the effusive honeysuckles and in the illusory depths of the mirrors. In his lifetime, he suffered from unreality, as do so many Englishmen; once dead, he is not even the ghost he was then. He was tall and listless and his tired rectangular beard had once then been red. I understand he was a widower, without children. Every few years he would go to England, to visit (I judge from some photographs he showed us) a sundial and a few oaks. He and my father had entered into one of those close (the adjective is excessive) English friendships that begin by excluding confidences and very soon dispense with dialogue. They used to carry out an exchange of books and newspapers and engage in taciturn chess games . . . I remember him in the hotel corridor, with a mathematics book in his hand, sometimes looking at the irrecoverable colors of the sky. One afternoon, we spoke of the duodecimal system of numbering (in which twelve is written as 10). Ashe said that he was converting some kind of tables from the duodecimal to the sexagesimal system (in which sixty is written as 10). He added that the task had been entrusted to him by a Norwegian, in Rio Grande do Sul. We had known him for eight years and he had never mentioned his sojourn in that region . . . We talked of country life of the *capangas,* of the Brazilian etymology of the word *gaucho* (which some old Uruguayans still pronounce *gaúcho*) and nothing more was said—may God forgive me—of duodecimal functions. In September of 1937 (we were not at the hotel), Herbert Ashe died of a ruptured aneurysm. A few days before, he had received a sealed and certified package from Brazil. It was a book in large octavo. Ashe left it at the bar, where—months later—I found it. I began to leaf through it and experienced an astonished and airy feeling of vertigo which I shall not describe, for this is not the story of my emotions but of Uqbar and Tlön and Orbis Tertius. On one of the nights of Islam called the Night of Nights, the secret doors of heaven open wide and the water in the jars becomes sweeter; if those doors opened, I would not feel what I felt that afternoon. The book was written in English and contained 1001 pages. On the yellow leather back I read these curious words which were repeated on the title page: *A First Encyclopaedia of Tlön. Vol. XI. Hlaer to Jangr.* There was no indication of date or place. On the first page and on a leaf of silk paper that covered one of the color plates there was stamped a blue oval with this inscription: *Orbis Tertius.* Two years before I had discovered, in a volume of a certain pirated encyclopedia, a superficial description

16

of a nonexistent country; now chance afforded me something more precious and arduous. Now I held in my hands a vast methodical fragment of an unknown planet's entire history, with its architecture and its playing cards, with the dread of its mythologies and the murmur of its languages, with its emperors and its seas, with its minerals and its birds and its fish, with its algebra and its fire, with its theological and metaphysical controversy. And all of it articulated, coherent, with no visible doctrinal intent or tone of parody.

In the "Eleventh Volume" which I have mentioned, there are allusions to preceding and succeeding volumes. In an article in the *N. R. F.* which is now classic, Néstor Ibarra has denied the existence of those companion volumes; Ezequiel Martínez Estrada and Drieu La Rochelle have refuted that doubt, perhaps victoriously. The fact is that up to now the most diligent inquiries have been fruitless. In vain we have upended the libraries of the two Americas and of Europe. Alfonso Reyes, tired of these subordinate sleuthing procedures, proposes that we should all undertake the task of reconstructing the many and weighty tomes that are lacking: *ex ungue leonem.* He calculates, half in earnest and half jokingly, that a generation of *tlönistas* should be sufficient. This venturesome computation brings us back to the fundamental problem: Who are the inventors of Tlön? The plural is inevitable, because the hypothesis of a lone inventor—an infinite Leibniz laboring away darkly and modestly—has been unanimously discounted. It is conjectured that this brave new world is the work of a secret society of astronomers, biologists, engineers, metaphysicians, poets, chemists, algebraists, moralists, painters, geometers . . . directed by an obscure man of genius. Individuals mastering these diverse disciplines are abundant, but not so those capable of inventiveness and less so those capable of subordinating that inventiveness to a rigorous and systematic plan. This plan is so vast that each writer's contribution is infinitesimal. At first it was believed that Tlön was a mere chaos, an irresponsible license of the imagination; now it is known that it is a cosmos and that the intimate laws which govern it have been formulated, at least provisionally. Let it suffice for me to recall that the apparent contradictions of the Eleventh Volume are the fundamental basis for the proof that the other volumes exist, so lucid and exact is the order observed in it. The popular magazines, with pardonable excess, have spread news of the zoology and topography of Tlön; I think its transparent tigers and towers of blood perhaps do not merit the continued attention of *all* men. I shall venture to request a few minutes to expound its concept of the universe.

Hume noted for all time that Berkeley's arguments did not admit the slightest refutation nor did they cause the slightest conviction. This dictum is entirely correct in its application to the earth, but entirely false in Tlön. The nations of this planet are congenitally idealist. Their language and the derivations of their language—religion, letters, metaphysics—all presuppose idealism. The world for them is not a concourse of objects in space; it is a heterogeneous series of independent acts. It is successive and temporal, not spatial. There are no nouns in Tlön conjectural *Ursprache,* from which the "present" languages and the dialects are derived: there are impersonal verbs, modified by monosyllabic suffixes (or prefixes) with an adverbial value. For example: there is no word corresponding to the word "moon," but there is a verb which in English would be "to moon" or "to moonate." "The moon rose above the river" is *hlör u fang axaxaxas mlö,* or literally: "upward behind the onstreaming it mooned."

The preceding applies to the languages of the southern

hemisphere. In those of the northern hemisphere (on whose *Ursprache* there is very little data in the Eleventh Volume) the prime unit is not the verb, but the monosyllabic adjective. The noun is formed by an accumulation of adjectives. They do not say "moon," but rather "round airy-light on dark" or "pale-orange-of-the-sky" or any other such combination. In the example selected the mass of objectives refers to a real object, but this is purely fortuitous. The literature of this hemisphere (like Meinong's subsistent world) abounds in ideal objects, which are convoked and dissolved in a moment, according to poetic needs. At times they are determined by mere simultaneity. There are objects composed of two terms, one of visual and another of auditory character: the color of the rising sun and the faraway cry of a bird. There are objects of many terms: the sun and the water on a swimmer's chest, the vague tremulous rose color we see with our eyes closed, the sensation of being carried along by a river and also by sleep. These second-degree objects can be combined with others; through the use of certain abbreviations, the process is practically infinite. There are famous poems made up of one enormous word. This word forms a *poetic object* created by the author. The fact that no one believes in the reality of nouns paradoxically causes their number to be unending. The languages of Tlön's northern hemisphere contain all the nouns of the Indo-European languages—and many others as well.

It is no exaggeration to state that the classic culture of Tlön comprises only one discipline: psychology. All others are subordinated to it. I have said that the men of this planet conceive the universe as a series of mental processes which do not develop in space but successively in time. Spinoza ascribes to his inexhaustible divinity the attributes of extension and thought; no one on Tlön would understand the juxtaposition of the first (which is typical only of certain states) and the second—which is a perfect synonym of the cosmos. In other words, they do not conceive that the spatial persists in time. The perception of a cloud of smoke on the horizon and then of the burning field and then of the half-extinguished cigarette that produced the blaze is considered an example of association of ideas.

This monism or complete idealism invalidates all science. If we explain (or judge) a fact, we connect it with another; such linking, in Tlön, is a later state of the subject which cannot affect or illuminate the previous state. Every mental state is irreducible: the mere fact of naming it—i.e., of classifying it— implies a falsification. From which it can be deduced that there are no sciences on Tlön, not even reasoning. The paradoxical truth is that they do exist, and in almost uncountable number. The same thing happens with philosophies as happens with nouns in the northern hemisphere. The fact that every philosophy is by definition a dialectical game, a *Philosophie des Als Ob,* has caused them to multiply. There is an abundance of incredible systems of pleasing design or sensational type. The metaphysicians of Tlön do not seek for the truth or even for verisimilitude, but rather for the astounding. They judge that metaphysics is a branch of fantastic literature. They know that a system is nothing more than the subordination of all aspects of the universe to any one such aspect. Even the phrase "all aspects" is rejectable, for it supposes the impossible addition of the present and of all past moments. Neither is it licit to use the plural "past moments," since it supposes another impossible operation . . . One of the schools of Tlön goes so far as to negate time: it reasons that the present is indefinite, that the future has no reality other than as a present hope, that the past has no reality other than as a present memory.[1] Another school declares that *all time* has already transpired and that our life is only the crepuscular and no doubt falsified and mutilated memory or reflection of an irrecoverable process. Another, that the history of the universe—and in it our lives and the most tenuous detail of our lives—is the scripture produced by a subordinate god in order to communicate with a demon. Another, that the universe is comparable to those cryptographs in which not all the symbols are valid and that only what happens every three hundred nights is true. Another, that while we sleep here, we are awake elsewhere and that in this way every man is two men.

Amongst the doctrines of Tlön, none has merited the scandalous reception accorded to materialism. Some thinkers have formulated it with less clarity than fervor, as one might put forth a paradox. In order to facilitate the comprehension of this inconceivable thesis, a heresiarch of the eleventh century[2] devised the sophism of the nine copper coins, whose scandalous renown is in Tlön equivalent to that of the Eleatic paradoxes. There are many versions of this "specious reasoning," which vary the number of coins and the number of discoveries; the following is the most common:

On Tuesday, X crosses a deserted road and loses nine copper coins. On Thursday, Y finds in the road four coins, somewhat rusted by Wednesday's rain. On Friday, Z discovers three coins in the road. On Friday morning, X finds two coins in the corridor of this house. The heresiarch would deduce from this story the reality—i.e., the continuity—of the nine coins which were

---

[1]Russell (*The Analysis of Mind*, 1921, page 159) supposes that the planet has been created a few minutes ago, furnished with a humanity that "remembers" an illusory past.

[2]A century, according to the duodecimal system, signifies a period of a hundred and forty-four years.

recovered. *It is absurd* (he affirmed) *to imagine that four of the coins have not existed between Tuesday and Thursday, three between Tuesday and Friday afternoon, two between Tuesday and Friday morning. It is logical to think that they have existed—at least in some secret way, hidden from the comprehension of men— at every moment of those three periods.*

The language of Tlön resists the formulation of this paradox; most people did not even understand it. The defenders of common sense at first did no more than negate the veracity of the anecdote. They repeated that it was a verbal fallacy, based on the rash application of two neologisms not authorized by usage and alien to all rigorous thought: the verbs "find" and "lose," which beg the question, because they presuppose the identity of the first and of the last nine coins. They recalled that all nouns (man, coin, Thursday, Wednesday, rain) have only a metaphorical value. They denounced the treacherous circumstance "somewhat rusted by Wednesday's rain," which presupposes what is trying to be demonstrated: the persistence of the four coins from Tuesday to Thursday. They explained that *equality* is one thing and *identity* another, and formulated a kind of *reductio ad absurdum:* the hypothetical case of nine men who on nine successive nights suffer a severe pain. Would it not be ridiculous—they questioned—to pretend that this pain is one and the same?[1] They said that the heresiarch was prompted only by the blasphemous intention of attributing the divine category of *being* to some simple coins and that at times he negated plurality and at other times did not. They

[1] Today, one of the churches of Tlön Platonically maintains that a certain pain, a certain greenish tint of yellow, a certain temperature, a certain sound, are the only reality. All men, in the vertiginous moment of coitus, are the same man. All men who repeat a line from Shakespeare *are* William Shakespeare.

argued: if equality implies identity, one would also have to admit that the nine coins are one.

Unbelievably, these refutations were not definitive. A hundred years after the problem was stated, a thinker no less brilliant than the heresiarch but of orthodox tradition formulated a very daring hypothesis. This happy conjecture affirmed that there is only one subject, that this indivisible subject is every being in the universe and that these beings are the organs and masks of the divinity. X is Y and is Z. Z discovers three coins because he remembers that X lost them; X finds two in the corridor because he remembers that the others have been found . . . The Eleventh Volume suggests that three prime reasons determined the complete victory of this idealist pantheism. The first, its repudiation of solipsism; the second, the possibility of preserving the psychological basis of the sciences; the third, the possibility of preserving the cult of the gods. Schopenhauer (the passionate and lucid Schopenhauer) formulates a very similar doctrine in the first volume of *Parerga und Paralipomena*.

The geometry of Tlön comprises two somewhat different disciplines: the visual and the tactile. The latter corresponds to our own geometry and is subordinated to the first. The basis of visual geometry is the surface, not the point. This geometry disregards parallel lines and declares that man in his movement modifies the forms which surround him. The basis of its arithmetic is the notion of indefinite numbers. They emphasize the importance of the concepts of greater and lesser, which our mathematicians symbolize as > and <. They maintain that the operation of counting modifies quantities and converts them from indefinite into definite sums. The fact that several individuals who count the same quantity should obtain the same result is, for the psychologists, an example of association of ideas or of a good exercise of memory. We already know that in Tlön the subject of knowledge is one and eternal.

In literary practices the ideas of a single subject is also all-powerful. It is uncommon for books to be signed. The concept of plagiarism does not exist: it has been established that all works are the creation of one author, who is atemporal and anonymous. The critics often invent authors: they select two dissimilar works—the *Tao Te Ching* and the *1001 Nights,* say—attribute them to the same writer and then determine most scrupulously the psychology of this interesting *homme de lettres* . . .

Their books are also different. Works of fiction contain a single plot, with all its imaginable permutations. Those of a philosophical nature invariably include both the thesis and the antithesis, the rigorous pro and con of a doctrine. A book which does not contain its counterbook is considered incomplete.

Centuries and centuries of idealism have not failed to influence reality. In the most ancient regions of Tlön, the duplication of lost objects is not infrequent. Two persons look for a pencil; the first finds it and says nothing; the second finds a second pencil, no less real, but closer to his expectations. These secondary objects are called *hrönir* and are, though awkward in form, somewhat longer. Until recently, the *hrönir* were the accidental products of distraction and forgetfulness. It seems unbelievable that their methodical production dates back scarcely a hundred years, but this is what the Eleventh Volume tells us. The first efforts were unsuccessful. However, the *modus operandi* merits description. The director of one of the state prisons told his inmates that there were certain tombs in an ancient river bed and promised freedom to whoever might make an important discovery. During the months preceding the excavation the inmates were shown photographs of what they were to find. This first effort proved that expectation and anxiety can be inhibitory; a week's work with pick and shovel did not manage to unearth anything in the way of a *hrön* except a rusty wheel of a period posterior to the experiment. But this was kept in secret and the process was repeated later in four schools. In three of them the failure was almost complete; in the fourth (whose director died accidentally during the first excavations) the students unearthed—or produced—a gold mask, an archaic sword, two or three clay urns and the moldy and mutilated torso of a king whose chest bore an inscription which it has not yet been possible to decipher. Thus was discovered the unreliability of witnesses who knew of the experimental nature of the search . . . Mass investigations produce contradictory objects; now individual and almost improvised jobs are preferred. The methodical fabrication of *hrönir* (says the Eleventh Volume) has performed prodigious services for archaeologists. It has made possible the interrogation and even the modification of the past, which is now no less plastic and docile than the future. Curiously, the *hrönir* of second and third degree—the *hrönir* derived from another *hrön,* those derived from the *hrön* of a *hrön*—exaggerate the aberrations of the initial one; those of fifth degree are almost uniform; those of ninth degree become confused with those of the second; in those of the eleventh there is a purity of line not found in the original. The process is cyclical: the *hrön* of twelfth degree begins to fall off in quality. Stranger and more pure than any *hrön* is, at times, the *ur:* the object produced through suggestion, educed by hope. The great golden mask I have mentioned is an illustrious example.

Things become duplicated in Tlön; they also tend to become effaced and lose their details when they are forgotten. A classic example is the doorway which survived so long as it was visited by a beggar and disappeared at his death.

At times some birds, a horse, have saved the ruins of an amphitheater.

Postscript (1947). I reproduce the preceding article just as it appeared in the *Anthology of Fantastic Literature* (1940), with no omission other than that of a few metaphors and a kind of sarcastic summary which now seems frivolous. So many things have happened since then . . . I shall do no more than recall them here.

In March of 1941 a letter written by Gunnar Erfjord was discovered in a book by Hinton which had belonged to Herbert Ashe. The envelope bore a cancellation from Ouro Preto; the letter completely elucidated the mystery of Tlön. Its text corroborated the hypotheses of Martínez Estrada. One night in Lucerne or in London, in the early seventeenth century, the splendid history has its beginning. A secret and benevolent society (amongst whose members were Dalgarno and later George Berkeley) arose to invent a country. Its vague initial program included "hermetic studies," philanthropy and the cabala. From this first period dates the curious book by Andreä. After a few years of secret conclaves and premature syntheses it was understood that one generation was not sufficient to give articulate form to a country. They resolved that each of the masters should elect a disciple who would continue his work. This hereditary arrangement prevailed; after an interval of two centuries the persecuted fraternity sprang up again in America. In 1824, in Memphis (Tennessee), one of its affiliates conferred with the ascetic millionaire Ezra Buckley. The latter, somewhat disdainfully, let him speak—and laughed at the plan's modest scope. He told the agent that in America it was absurd to invent a country and proposed the invention of a planet. To this gigantic idea he added another, a product of his nihilism:[1] that of keeping the enormous enterprise secret. At that time the twenty volumes of the *Encyclopaedia Britannica* were circulating in the United States; Buckley suggested that a methodical encyclopedia of the imaginary planet be written. He was to leave them his mountains of gold, his navigable rivers, his pasture lands roamed by cattle and buffalo, his Negroes, his brothels and his dollars, on one condition: "The work will make no pact with the impostor Jesus Christ." Buckley did not believe in God, but he wanted to demonstrate to this nonexistent God that mortal man was capable of conceiving a world. Buckley was poisoned in Baton Rouge in 1828; in 1914 the society delivered to its collaborators, some three hundred in number, the last volume of the First Encyclopedia of Tlön. The edition was a secret one; its forty volumes (the vastest undertaking ever carried out by man) would be the basis for another more detailed edition, written not in English but in one of the languages of Tlön. This revision of an illusory world, was called, provisionally, *Orbis Tertius* and one of its modest demiurgi was Herbert Ashe, whether as an agent of Gunnar Erfjord or as an affiliate, I do not know. His having received a copy of the Eleventh Volume would seem to favor the latter assumption. But what about the others?

In 1942 events became more intense. I recall one of the first of these with particular clarity and it seems that I perceived then something of its premonitory character. It happened in an apartment on Laprida Street, facing a high and light balcony which looked out toward the sunset. Princess Faucigny Lucinge had received her silverware from Poitiers. From the vast depths of a box embellished with foreign stamps, delicate immobile objects emerged: silver from Utrecht and Paris cov-

[1]Buckley was a freethinker, a fatalist and a defender of slavery.

ered with hard heraldic fauna, and a samovar. Amongst them—with the perceptible and tenuous tremor of a sleeping bird—a compass vibrated mysteriously. The Princess did not recognize it. Its blue needle longed for magnetic north; its metal case was concave in shape; the letters around its edge corresponded to one of the alphabets of Tlön. Such was the first intrusion of this fantastic world into the world of reality.

I am still troubled by a stroke of chance which made me the witness of the second intrusion as well. It happened some months later, at a country store owned by a Brazilian in Cuchilla Negra. Amorim and I were returning from Sant' Anna. The River Tacuarembó had flooded and we were obliged to sample (and endure) the proprietor's rudimentary hospitality. He provided us with some creaking cots in a large room cluttered with barrels and hides. We went to bed, but were kept from sleeping until dawn by the drunken ravings of an unseen neighbor, who intermingled inextricable insults with snatches of *milongas*—or rather with snatches of the same *milonga*. As might be supposed, we attributed this insistent uproar to the store owner's fiery cane liquor. By daybreak, the man was dead in the hallway. The roughness of his voice had deceived us: he was only a youth. In his delirium a few coins had fallen from his belt, along with a cone of bright metal, the size of a die. In vain a boy tried to pick up this cone. A man was scarcely able to raise it from the ground. I held it in my hand for a few minutes; I remember that its weight was intolerable and that after it was removed, the feeling of oppressiveness remained. I also remember the exact circle it pressed into my palm. This sensation of a very small and at the same time extremely heavy object produced a disagreeable impression of repugnance and fear. One of the local men suggested we throw it into the swollen river; Amorim acquired it for a few pesos. No one knew anything about the dead man, except that "he came from the border." These small, very heavy cones (made from a metal which is not of this world) are images of the divinity in certain regions of Tlön.

Here I bring the personal part of my narrative to a close. The rest is in the memory (if not in the hopes or fears) of all my readers. Let it suffice for me to recall or mention the following facts, with a mere brevity of words which the reflective recollection of all will enrich or amplify. Around 1944, a person doing research for the newspaper *The American* (of Nashville, Tennessee) brought to light in a Memphis library the forty volumes of the First Encyclopedia of Tlön. Even today there is a controversy over whether this discovery was accidental or whether it was permitted by the directors of the still nebulous *Orbis Tertius*. The latter is most likely. Some of the incredible aspects of the Eleventh Volume (for example, the multiplication of the *hrönir*) have been eliminated or attenuated in the Memphis copies; it is reasonable to imagine that these omissions follow the plan of exhibiting a world which is not too incompatible with the real world. The dissemination of objects from Tlön over different countries would complement this plan . . .[1] The fact is that the international press infinitely proclaimed the "find." Manuals, anthologies, summaries, literal versions, authorized re-editions and pirated editions of the Greatest Work of Man flooded and still flood the earth. Almost immediately, reality yielded on more than one account. The truth is that it longed to yield. Ten years ago any symmetry with a semblance of order—dialectical materialism, anti-Semitism, Nazism—was sufficient to entrance the minds of men. How could one do other than submit to Tlön, to the minute and vast evidence of an orderly planet? It is use-

[1]There remains, of course, the problem of the *material* of some objects.

ess to answer that reality is also orderly. Perhaps it is, but in accordance with divine laws—I translate: inhuman laws—which we never quite grasp. Tlön is surely a labyrinth, but it is a labyrinth devised by men, a labyrinth destined to be deciphered by men.

The contact of the habit of Tlön have disintegrated this world. Enchanted by its vigor, humanity forgets over and again that it is a rigor of chess masters, not of angels. Already the schools have been invaded by the (conjectural) "primitive language" of Tlön; already the teaching of its harmonious history (filled with moving episodes) has wiped out the one which governed in my childhood; already a fictitious past occupies in our memories the place of another, a past of which we know nothing with certainty—not even that it is false. Numismatology, pharmacology and archaeology have been reformed. I understand that biology and mathematics also await their avatars . . . A scattered dynasty of solitary men has changed the face of the world. Their task continues. If our forecasts are not in error, a hundred years from now someone will discover the hundred volumes of the Second Encyclopedia of Tlön.

Then English and French and mere Spanish will disappear from the globe. The world will be Tlön. I pay no attention to all this and go on revising, in the still days at the Adrogué hotel, an uncertain Quevedian translation (which I do not intend to publish) of Browne's *Urn Burial*.

Translated by James E. Irby

The Lottery in Babylon

Like all men in Babylon, I have been proconsul; like all, a slave. I have also known omnipotence, opprobrium, imprisonment. Look: the index finger on my right hand is missing. Look: through the rip in my cape you can see a vermilion tattoo on my stomach. It is the second symbol, Beth. This letter, on nights when the moon is full, gives me power over men whose mark is Gimmel, but it subordinates me to the men of Aleph, who on moonless nights owe obedience to those marked with Gimmel. In the half light of dawn, in a cellar, I have cut the jugular vein of sacred bulls before a black stone. During a lunar year I have been declared invisible. I shouted and they did not answer me; I stole bread and they did not behead me. I have known what the Greeks do not know, incertitude. In a bronze chamber, before the silent handkerchief of the strangler, hope has been faithful to me, as has panic in the river of pleasure. Heraclides Ponticus tells with amazement that Pythagoras remembered having been Pyrrhus and before that Euphorbus and before that some other mortal. In order to remember similar vicissitudes I do not need to have recourse to death or even to deception.

I owe this almost atrocious variety to an institution which other republics do not know or which operates in them in an imperfect and secret manner: the lottery. I have not looked into its history; I know that the wise men cannot agree. I

31

know of its powerful purposes what a man who is not versed in astrology can know about the moon. I come from a dizzy land where the lottery is the basis of reality. Until today I have thought as little about it as I have about the conduct of indecipherable divinities or about my heart. Now, far from Babylon and its beloved customs, I think with a certain amount of amazement about the lottery and about the blasphemous conjectures which veiled men murmur in the twilight.

My father used to say that formerly—a matter of centuries, of years?—the lottery in Babylon was a game of plebeian character. He recounted (I don't know whether rightly) that barbers sold, in exchange for copper coins, squares of bone or of parchment adorned with symbols. In broad daylight a drawing took place. Those who won received silver coins without any other test of luck. The system was elementary, as you can see.

Naturally these "lotteries" failed. Their moral virtue was nil. They were not directed at all of man's faculties, but only at hope. In the face of public indifference, the merchants who founded these venal lotteries began to lose money. Someone tried a reform: The interpolation of a few unfavorable tickets in the list of favorable numbers. By means of this reform, the buyers of numbered squares ran the double risk of winning a sum and of paying a fine that could be considerable. This slight danger (for every thirty favorable numbers there was one unlucky one) awoke, as is natural, the interest of the public. The Babylonians threw themselves into the game. Those who did not acquire chances were considered pusillanimous, cowardly. In time, that justified disdain was doubled. Those who did not play were scorned, but also the losers who paid the fine were scorned. The Company (as it came to be known then) had to take care of the winners, who could not cash in their prizes if almost the total amount of the fines was unpaid.

It started a lawsuit against the losers. The judge condemned them to pay the original fine and costs or spend several days in jail. All chose jail in order to defraud the Company. The bravado of a few is the source of the omnipotence of the Company and of its metaphysical and ecclesiastical power.

A little while afterward the lottery lists omitted the amounts of fines and limited themselves to publishing the days of imprisonment that each unfavorable number indicated. That laconic spirit, almost unnoticed at the time, was of capital importance. *It was the first appearance in the lottery of nonmonetary elements.* The success was tremendous. Urged by the clientele, the Company was obliged to increase the unfavorable numbers.

Everyone knows that the people of Babylon are fond of logic and even of symmetry. It was illogical for the lucky numbers to be computed in round coins and the unlucky ones in days and nights of imprisonment. Some moralists reasoned that the possession of money does not always determine happiness and that other forms of happiness are perhaps more direct.

Another concern swept the quarters of the poorer classes. The members of the college of priests multiplied their stakes and enjoyed all the vicissitudes of terror and hope; the poor (with reasonable or unavoidable envy) knew that they were excluded from that notoriously delicious rhythm. The just desire that all, rich and poor, should participate equally in the lottery, inspired an indignant agitation, the memory of which the years have not erased. Some obstinate people did not understand (or pretended not to understand) that it was a question of a new order, of a necessary historical stage. A slave stole a crimson ticket, which in the drawing credited him with the burning of his tongue. The legal code fixed that same penalty for the one who stole a ticket. Some Babylonians argued that he deserved the burning irons in his status of a thief; others, generously, that the executioner should apply it to him because chance had determined it that way. There were disturbances, there were lamentable drawings of blood, but the masses of Babylon finally imposed their will against the opposition of the rich. The people achieved amply its generous purposes. In the first place, it caused the Company to accept total power. (That unification was necessary, given the vastness and complexity of the new operations.) In the second place, it made the lottery secret, free and general. The mercenary sale of chances was abolished. Once initiated in the mysteries of Baal, every free man automatically participated in the sacred drawings, which took place in the labyrinths of the god every sixty nights and which determined his destiny until the next drawing. The consequences were incalculable. A fortunate play could bring about his promotion to the council of wise men or the imprisonment of an enemy (public or private) or finding, in the peaceful darkness of his room, the woman who begins to excite him and whom he never expected to see again. A bad play: mutilation, different kinds of infamy, death. At times one single fact—the vulgar murder of C, the mysterious apotheosis of B—was the happy solution of thirty or forty drawings. To combine the plays was difficult, but one must remember that the individuals of the Company were (and are) omnipotent and astute. In many cases the knowledge that certain happinesses were the simple product of chance would have diminished their virtue. To avoid that obstacle, the agents of the Company made use of the power of suggestion and magic. Their steps, their maneuverings, were secret. To find out about the intimate hopes and terrors of each individual, they had astrologists and spies. There were certain stone lions, there was a sacred latrine called Qaphqa, there were fissures in a dusty aqueduct which, according to general

34

opinion, *led to the Company;* malignant or benevolent persons deposited information in these places. An alphabetical file collected these items of varying truthfulness.

Incredibly, there were complaints. The Company, with its usual discretion, did not answer directly. It preferred to scrawl in the rubbish of a mask factory a brief statement which now figures in the sacred scriptures. This doctrinal item observed that the lottery is an interpolation of chance in the order of the world and that to accept errors is not to contradict chance: it is to corroborate it. It likewise observed that those lions and that sacred receptacle, although not disavowed by the Company (which did not abandon the right to consult them), functioned without official guarantee.

This declaration pacified the public's restlessness. It also produced other effects, perhaps unforeseen by its writer. It deeply modified the spirit and the operations of the Company. I don't have much time left; they tell us that the ship is about to weigh anchor. But I shall try to explain it.

However unlikely it might seem, no one had tried out before then a general theory of chance. Babylonians are not very speculative. They revere the judgments of fate, they deliver to them their lives, their hopes, their panic, but it does not occur to them to investigate fate's labyrinthine laws nor the gyratory spheres which reveal it. Nevertheless, the *unofficial* declaration that I have mentioned inspired many discussions of judicial-mathematical character. From some one of them the following conjecture was born: If the lottery is an intensification of chance, a periodical infusion of chaos in the cosmos, would it not be right for chance to intervene in all stages of the drawing and not in one alone? Is it not ridiculous for chance to dictate someone's death and have the circumstances of that death—secrecy, publicity, the fixed time of an hour or a century—not subject to chance? These just scruples finally caused a considerable reform, whose complexities (aggravated by centuries' practice) only a few specialists understand, but which I shall try to summarize, at least in a symbolic way.

Let us imagine a first drawing, which decrees the death of a man. For its fulfillment one proceeds to another drawing, which proposes (let us say) nine possible executors. Of these executors, four can initiate a third drawing which will tell the name of the executioner, two can replace the adverse order with a fortunate one (finding a treasure, let us say), another will intensify the death penalty (that is, will make it infamous or enrich it with tortures), others can refuse to fulfill it. This is the symbolic scheme. In reality *the number of drawings is infinite*. No decision is final, all branch into others. Ignorant people suppose that infinite drawings require an infinite time; actually it is sufficient for time to be infinitely subdivisible, as the famous parable of the contest with the tortoise teaches. This infinity harmonizes admirably with the sinuous numbers of Chance and with the Celestial Archetype of the Lottery, which the Platonists adore. Some warped echo of our rites seems to have resounded on the Tiber: Ellus Lampridius, in the *Life of Antoninus Heliogabalus,* tells that this emperor wrote on shells the lots that were destined for his guests, so that one received ten pounds of gold and another ten flies, ten dormice, ten bears. It is permissible to recall that Heliogabalus was brought up in Asia Minor, among the priests of the eponymous god.

There are also impersonal drawings, with an indefinite purpose. One decrees that a sapphire of Taprobana be thrown into the waters of the Euphrates; another, that a bird be released from the roof of a tower; another, that each century there be withdrawn (or added) a grain of sand from the innumerable ones on the beach. The consequences are, at times, terrible.

Under the beneficent influence of the Company, our customs are saturated with chance. The buyer of a dozen amphoras of Damascene wine will not be surprised if one of them contains a talisman or a snake. The scribe who writes a contract almost never fails to introduce some erroneous information. I myself, in this hasty declaration, have falsified some splendor, some atrocity. Perhaps, also, some mysterious monotony . . . Our historians, who are the most penetrating on the globe, have invented a method to correct chance. It is well known that the operations of this method are (in general) reliable, although, naturally, they are not divulged without some portion of deceit. Furthermore, there is nothing so contaminated with fiction as the history of the Company. A paleographic document, exhumed in a temple, can be the result of yesterday's lottery or of an age-old lottery. No book is published without some discrepancy in each one of the copies. Scribes take a secret oath to omit, to interpolate, to change. The indirect lie is also cultivated.

The Company, with divine modesty, avoids all publicity. Its agents, as is natural, are secret. The orders which it issues continually (perhaps incessantly) do not differ from those lavished by impostors. Moreover, who can brag about being a mere impostor? The drunkard who improvises an absurd order, the dreamer who awakens suddenly and strangles the woman who sleeps at his side, do they not execute, perhaps, a secret decision of the Company? That silent functioning, comparable to God's, gives rise to all sorts of conjectures. One abominably insinuates that the Company has not existed for centuries and that the sacred disorder of our lives is purely hereditary, traditional. Another judges it eternal and teaches that it will last until the last night, when the last god annihilates the world. Another declares that the Company is omnipotent, but that it only has influence in tiny things: in a bird's call, in the shadings of rust and of dust, in the half dreams of dawn. Another, in the words of masked heresiarchs, *that it has never existed and will not exist.* Another, no less vile, reasons that it is indifferent to affirm or deny the reality of the shadowy corporation, because Babylon is nothing else than an infinite game of chance.

Translated by John M. Fein

The Garden of Forking Paths

On page 22 of Liddell Hart's *History of World War I* you will read that an attack against the Serre-Montauban line by thirteen British divisions (supported by 1,400 artillery pieces), planned for the 24th of July, 1916, had to be postponed until the morning of the 29th. The torrential rains, Captain Liddell Hart comments, caused this delay, an insignificant one, to be sure.

The following statement, dictated, reread and signed by Dr. Yu Tsun, former professor of English at the *Hochschule* at Tsingtao, throws an unsuspected light over the whole affair. The first two pages of the document are missing.

". . . and I hung up the receiver. Immediately afterwards, I recognized the voice that had answered in German. It was that of Captain Richard Madden. Madden's presence in Viktor Runeberg's apartment meant the end of our anxieties and—but this seemed, *or should have seemed,* very secondary to me—also the end of our lives. It meant that Runeberg had been arrested or murdered.[1] Before the sun set on that day, I

[1] An hypothesis both hateful and odd. The Prussian spy Hans Rabener, alias Viktor Runeberg, attacked with drawn automatic the bearer of the warrant for his arrest, Captain Richard Madden. The latter, in self-defense, inflicted the wound which brought about Runeberg's death. (Editor's note.)

would encounter the same fate. Madden was implacable. Or rather, he was obliged to be so. An Irishman at the service of England, a man accused of laxity and perhaps of treason, how could he fail to seize and be thankful for such a miraculous opportunity: the discovery, capture, maybe even the death of two agents of the German Reich? I went up to my room; absurdly I locked the door and threw myself on my back on the narrow iron cot. Through the window I saw the familiar roofs and the cloud-shaded six o'clock sun. It seemed incredible to me that that day without premonitions or symbols should be the one of my inexorable death. In spite of my dead father, in spite of having been a child in a symmetrical garden of Hai Feng, was I—now—going to die? Then I reflected that everything happens to a man precisely, precisely *now*. Centuries of centuries and only in the present do things happen; countless men in the air, on the face of the earth and the sea, and all that really is happening is happening to me . . . The almost intolerable recollection of Madden's horselike face banished these wanderings. In the midst of my hatred and terror (it means nothing to me now to speak of terror, now that I have mocked Richard Madden, now that my throat yearns for the noose) it occurred to me that that tumultuous and doubtless happy warrior did not suspect that I possessed the Secret. The name of the exact location of the new British artillery park on the River Ancre. A bird streaked across the gray sky and blindly I translated it into an airplane and that airplane into many (against the French sky) annihilating the artillery station with vertical bombs. If only my mouth, before a bullet shattered it, could cry out that secret name so it could be heard in Germany . . . My human voice was very weak. How might I make it carry to the ear of the Chief? To the ear of that sick and hateful man who knew nothing of Runeberg and me save that we were in Staffordshire and who was waiting in vain for our report in his arid office in Berlin, endlessly examining newspapers . . . I said out loud: *I must flee.* I sat up noiselessly, in a useless perfection of silence, as if Madden were already lying in wait for me. Something—perhaps the mere vain ostentation of proving my resources were nil— made me look through my pockets. I found what I knew I would find. The American watch, the nickel chain and the square coin, the key ring with the incriminating useless keys to Runeberg's apartment, the notebook, a letter which I re- solved to destroy immediately (and which I did not destroy), a crown, two shillings and a few pence, the red and blue pencil, the handkerchief, the revolver with one bullet. Absurdly, I took it in my hand and weighed it in order to inspire courage within myself. Vaguely I thought that a pistol report can be heard at a great distance. In ten minutes my plan was per- fected. The telephone book listed the name of the only person capable of transmitting the message; he lived in a suburb of Fenton, less than a half hour's train ride away.

I am a cowardly man. I say it now, now that I have carried to its end a plan whose perilous nature no one can deny. I know its execution was terrible. I didn't do it for Germany, no. I care nothing for a barbarous country which imposed upon me the abjection of being a spy. Besides, I know of a man from England—a modest man—who for me is no less great than Goethe. I talked with him for scarcely an hour, but dur- ing that hour he was Goethe . . . I did it because I sensed that the Chief somehow feared people of my race—for the in- numerable ancestors who merge within me. I wanted to prove to him that a yellow man could save his armies. Besides, I had to flee from Captain Madden. His hands and his voice could call at my door at any moment. I dressed silently, bade farewell to myself in the mirror, went downstairs, scrutinized the peaceful street and went out. The station was not far from my home, but I judged it wise to take a cab. I argued that in this way I ran less risk of being recognized; the fact is that in the deserted street I felt myself visible and vulnerable, infinitely so. I remember that I told the cab driver to stop a short distance before the main entrance. I got out with voluntary, almost painful slowness; I was going to the village of Ashgrove but I bought a ticket for a more distant station. The train left within a very few minutes, at eight-fifty. I hurried; the next one would leave at nine-thirty. There was hardly a soul on the platform. I went through the coaches; I remember a few farmers, a woman dressed in mourning, a young boy who was reading with fervor the *Annals* of Tacitus, a wounded and happy soldier. The coaches jerked forward at last. A man whom I recognized ran in vain to the end of the platform. It was Captain Richard Madden. Shattered, trembling, I shrank into the far corner of the seat, away from the dreaded window.

From this broken state I passed into an almost abject felicity. I told myself that the duel had already begun and that I had won the first encounter by frustrating, even if for forty minutes, even if by a stroke of fate, the attack of my adversary. I argued that this slightest of victories foreshadowed a total victory. I argued (no less fallaciously) that my cowardly felicity proved that I was a man capable of carrying out the adventure successfully. From this weakness I took strength that did not abandon me. I foresee that man will resign himself each day to more atrocious undertakings; soon there will be no one but warriors and brigands; I give them this counsel: *The author of an atrocious undertaking ought to imagine that he has already accomplished it, ought to impose upon himself a future as irrevocable as the past.* Thus I proceeded as my eyes of a man already dead registered the elapsing of that day, which was perhaps the last, and the diffusion of the night. The train ran gently along, amid ash trees. It stopped, almost in the middle of the fields.

No one announced the name of the station. "Ashgrove?" I asked a few lads on the platform. "Ashgrove," they replied. I got off.

A lamp enlightened the platform but the faces of the boys were in shadow. One questioned me, "Are you going to Dr. Stephen Albert's house?" Without waiting for my answer, another said, "The house is a long way from here, but you won't get lost if you take this road to the left and at every crossroads turn again to your left." I tossed them a coin (my last), descended a few stone steps and started down the solitary road. It went downhill, slowly. It was of elemental earth; overhead the branches were tangled; the low full moon seemed to accompany me.

For an instant, I thought that Richard Madden in some way had penetrated my desperate plan. Very quickly, I understood that that was impossible. The instructions to turn always to the left reminded me that such was the common procedure for discovering the central point of certain labyrinths. I have some understanding of labyrinths: not for nothing am I the great grandson of that Ts'ui Pên who was governor of Yunnan and who renounced worldly power in order to write a novel that might be even more populous than the *Hung Lu Meng* and to construct a labyrinth in which all men would become lost. Thirteen years he dedicated to these heterogeneous tasks, but the hand of a stranger murdered him—and his novel was incoherent and no one found the labyrinth. Beneath English trees I meditated on that lost maze: I imagined it inviolate and perfect at the secret crest of a mountain; I imagined it erased by rice fields or beneath the water; I imagined it infinite, no longer composed of octagonal kiosks and returning paths, but of rivers and provinces and kingdoms . . . I thought of a labyrinth of labyrinths, of one sinuous spreading labyrinth that would encompass the past and the future and in some way involve the stars. Absorbed in these illusory images, I forgot my destiny of one pursued. I felt myelf to be, for an unknown period of time, an abstract perceiver of the world. The vague, living countryside, the moon, the remains of the day worked on me, as well as the slope of the road which eliminated any possibility of weariness. The afternoon was intimate, infinite. The road descended and forked among the now confused meadows. A high-pitched, almost syllabic music approached and receded in the shifting of the wind, dimmed by leaves and distance. I thought that a man can be an enemy of other men, of the moments of other men, but not of a country: not of fireflies, words, gardens, streams of water, sunsets. Thus I arrived before a tall, rusty gate. Between the iron bars I made out a poplar grove and a pavilion. I understood suddenly two things, the first trivial, the second almost unbelievable: the music came from the pavilion, and the music was Chinese. For precisely that reason I had openly accepted it without paying it any heed. I do not remember whether there was a bell or whether I knocked with my hand. The sparkling of the music continued.

From the rear of the house within a lantern approached: a lantern that the trees sometimes striped and sometimes eclipsed, a paper lantern that had the form of a drum and the color of the moon. A tall man bore it. I didn't see his face for the light blinded me. He opened the door and said slowly, in my own language: "I see that the pious Hsi P'êng persists in correcting my solitude. You no doubt wish to see the garden?"

I recognized the name of one of our consuls and I replied, disconcerted, "The garden?"

"The garden of forking paths."

Something stirred in my memory and I uttered with incomprehensible certainty, "The garden of my ancestor Ts'ui Pên."

"Your ancestor? Your illustrious ancestor? Come in."

The damp path zigzagged like those of my childhood. We came to a library of Eastern and Western books. I recognized bound in yellow silk several volumes of the Lost Encyclopedia, edited by the Third Emperor of the Luminous Dynasty but never printed. The record on the phonograph revolved next to a bronze phoenix. I also recall a *famille rose* vase and another, many centuries older, of that shade of blue which our craftsmen copied from the potters of Persia . . .

Stephen Albert observed me with a smile. He was, as I have said, very tall, sharp-featured, with gray eyes and a gray beard. He told me that he had been a missionary in Tientsin "before aspiring to become a Sinologist."

We sat down—I on a long, low divan, he with his back to the window and a tall circular clock. I calculated that my pursuer, Richard Madden, could not arrive for at least an hour. My irrevocable determination could wait.

"An astounding fate, that of Ts'ui Pên," Stephen Albert said. "Governor of his native province, learned in astronomy, in astrology and in the tireless interpretation of the canonical books, chess player, famous poet and calligrapher—he abandoned all this in order to compose a book and a maze. He renounced the pleasures of both tyranny and justice, of his populous couch, of his banquets and even of erudition—all to close himself up for thirteen years in the Pavilion of the Limpid Solitude. When he died, his heirs found nothing save chaotic manuscripts. His family, as you may be aware, wished to condemn them to the fire; but his executor—a Taoist or Buddhist monk—insisted on their publication."

"We descendants of Ts'ui Pên," I replied, "continue to curse that monk. Their publication was senseless. The book is an indeterminate heap of contradictory drafts. I examined it once: in the third chapter the hero dies, in the fourth he

45

is alive. As for the other undertaking of Ts'ui Pên, his labyrinth . . ."

"Here is Ts'ui Pên's labyrinth," he said, indicating a tall lacquered desk.

"An ivory labyrinth!" I exclaimed. "A minimum labyrinth."

"A labyrinth of symbols," he corrected. "An invisible labyrinth of time. To me, a barbarous Englishman, has been entrusted the revelation of this diaphanous mystery. After more than a hundred years, the details are irretrievable; but it is not hard to conjecture what happened. Ts'ui Pên must have said once: *I am withdrawing to write a book.* And another time: *I am withdrawing to construct a labyrinth.* Every one imagined two works; to no one did it occur that the book and the maze were one and the same thing. The Pavilion of the Limpid Solitude stood in the center of a garden that was perhaps intricate; that circumstance could have suggested to the heirs a physical labyrinth. Ts'ui Pên died; no one in the vast territories that were his came upon the labyrinth; the confusion of the novel suggested to me that *it* was the maze. Two circumstances gave me the correct solution of the problem. One: the curious legend that Ts'ui Pên had planned to create a labyrinth which would be strictly infinite. The other: a fragment of a letter I discovered."

Albert rose. He turned his back on me for a moment; he opened a drawer of the black and gold desk. He faced me and in his hands he held a sheet of paper that had once been crimson, but was now pink and tenuous and cross-sectioned. The fame of Ts'ui Pên as a calligrapher had been justly won. I read, uncomprehendingly and with fervor, these words written with a minute brush by a man of my blood: *I leave to the various futures (not to all) my garden of forking paths.* Wordlessly, I returned the sheet. Albert continued:

46

"Before unearthing this letter, I had questioned myself about the ways in which a book can be infinite. I could think of nothing other than a cyclic volume, a circular one. A book whose last page was identical with the first, a book which had the possibility of continuing indefinitely. I remembered too that night which is at the middle of the Thousand and One Nights when Scheherazade (through a magical oversight of the copyist) begins to relate word for word the story of the Thousand and One Nights, establishing the risk of coming once again to the night when she must repeat it, and thus on to infinity. I imagined as well a Platonic, hereditary work, transmitted from father to son, in which each new individual adds a chapter or corrects with pious care the pages of his elders. These conjectures diverted me; but none seemed to correspond, not even remotely, to the contradictory chapters of Ts'ui Pên. In the midst of this perplexity, I received from Oxford the manuscript you have examined. I lingered, naturally, on the sentence: *I leave to the various futures (not to all) my garden of forking paths.* Almost instantly, I understood: 'the garden of forking paths' was the chaotic novel; the phrase 'the various futures (not to all)' suggested to me the forking in time, not in space. A broad rereading of the work confirmed the theory. In all fictional works, each time a man is confronted with several alternatives, he chooses one and eliminates the others; in the fiction of Ts'ui Pên, he chooses— simultaneously—all of them. *He creates,* in this way, diverse futures, diverse times which themselves also proliferate and fork. Here, then, is the explanation of the novel's contradictions. Fang, let us say, has a secret; a stranger calls at his door; Fang resolves to kill him. Naturally, there are several possible outcomes: Fang can kill the intruder, the intruder can kill Fang, they both can escape, they both can die, and so forth. In the work of Ts'ui Pên, all possible outcomes occur; each one is the point of departure for other forkings. Sometimes, the paths of this labyrinth converge: for example, you arrive at this house, but in one of the possible pasts you are my enemy, in another, my friend. If you will resign yourself to my incurable pronunciation, we shall read a few pages."

His face, within the vivid circle of the lamplight, was unquestionably that of an old man, but with something unalterable about it, even immortal. He read with slow precision two versions of the same epic chapter. In the first, an army marches to a battle across a lonely mountain; the horror of the rocks and shadows makes the men undervalue their lives and they gain an easy victory. In the second, the same army traverses a palace where a great festival is taking place; the resplendent battle seems to them a continuation of the celebration and they win the victory. I listened with proper veneration to these ancient narratives, perhaps less admirable in themselves than the fact that they had been created by my blood and were being restored to me by a man of a remote empire, in the course of a desperate adventure, on a Western isle. I remember the last words, repeated in each version like a secret commandment: *Thus fought the heroes, tranquil their admirable hearts, violent their swords, resigned to kill and to die.*

From that moment on, I felt about me and within my dark body an invisible, intangible swarming. Not the swarming of the divergent, parallel and finally coalescent armies, but a more inaccessible, more intimate agitation that they in some manner prefigured. Stephen Albert continued:

"I don't believe that your illustrious ancestor played idly with these variations. I don't consider it credible that he would sacrifice thirteen years to the infinite execution of a rhetorical experiment. In your country, the novel is a subsidiary form of literature; in Ts'ui Pên's time it was a despicable form. Ts'ui Pên was a brilliant novelist, but he was also a man of letters who doubtless did not consider himself a mere novelist. The testimony of his contemporaries proclaims—and his life fully confirms—his metaphysical and mystical interests. Philosophic controversy usurps a good part of the novel. I know that of all problems, none disturbed him so greatly nor worked upon him so much as the abysmal problem of time. Now then, the latter is the only problem that does not figure in the pages of the *Garden*. He does not even use the word that signifies *time*. How do you explain this voluntary omission?"

I proposed several solutions—all unsatisfactory. We discussed them. Finally, Stephen Albert said to me:

"In a riddle whose answer is chess, what is the only prohibited word?"

I thought a moment and replied, "The word *chess*."

"Precisely," said Albert. *"The Garden of Forking Paths* is an enormous riddle, or parable, whose theme is time; this recondite cause prohibits its mention. To omit a word always, to resort to inept metaphors and obvious periphrases, is perhaps the most emphatic way of stressing it. That is the tortuous method preferred, in each of the meanderings of his indefatigable novel, by the oblique Ts'ui Pên. I have compared hundreds of manuscripts, I have corrected the errors that the negligence of the copyists has introduced, I have guessed the plan of this chaos, I have re-established—I believe I have re-established—the primordial organization, I have translated the entire work: it is clear to me that not once does he employ the word 'time.' The explanation is obvious: *The Garden of Forking Paths* is an incomplete, but not false, image of the universe as Ts'ui Pên conceived it. In contrast to Newton and Schopenhauer, your ancestor did not believe in a uniform, absolute time. He believed in an infinite series of times, in a growing, dizzying net of divergent, convergent and parallel times. This network of times which approached one another, forked, broke off, or were unaware of one another for centuries, embraces *all* possibilities of time. We do not exist in the majority of these times; in some you exist, and not I; in others I, and not you; in others, both of us. In the present one, which a favorable fate has granted me, you have arrived at my house; in another, while crossing the garden, you found me dead; in still another, I utter these same words, but I am a mistake, a ghost."

"In every one," I pronounced, not without a tremble to my voice, "I am grateful to you and revere you for your re-creation of the garden of Ts'ui Pên."

"Not in all," he murmured with a smile. "Time forks perpetually toward innumerable futures. In one of them I am your enemy."

Once again I felt the swarming sensation of which I have spoken. It seemed to me that the humid garden that surrounded the house was infinitely saturated with invisible persons. Those persons were Albert and I, secret, busy and multiform in other dimensions of time. I raised my eyes and the tenuous nightmare dissolved. In the yellow and black garden there was only one man; but this man was as strong as a statue . . . this man was approaching along the path and he was Captain Richard Madden.

"The future already exists," I replied, "but I am your friend. Could I see the letter again?"

Albert rose. Standing tall, he opened the drawer of the tall desk; for the moment his back was to me. I had readied the revolver. I fired with extreme caution. Albert fell uncomplainingly, immediately. I swear his death was instantaneous—a lightning stroke.

The rest is unreal, insignificant. Madden broke in, arrested me. I have been condemned to the gallows. I have won out abominably; I have communicated to Berlin the secret name of the city they must attack. They bombed it yesterday; I read it in the same papers that offered to England the mystery of the learned Sinologist Stephen Albert who was murdered by a stranger, one Yu Tsun. The Chief had deciphered this mystery. He knew my problem was to indicate (through the uproar of the war) the city called Albert, and that I had found no other means to do so than to kill a man of that name. He does not know (no one can know) my innumerable contrition and weariness.

For Victoria Ocampo

Translated by Donald A. Yates

Death and the Compass

Of the many problems which exercised the reckless discernment of Lönnrot, none was so strange—so rigorously strange, shall we say—as the periodic series of bloody events which culminated at the villa of Triste-le-Roy, amid the ceaseless aroma of the eucalypti. It is true that Erik Lönnrot failed to prevent the last murder, but that he foresaw it is indisputable. Neither did he guess the identity of Yarmolinsky's luckless assassin, but he did succeed in divining the secret morphology behind the fiendish series as well as the participation of Red Scharlach, whose other nickname is Scharlach the Dandy. That criminal (as countless others) had sworn on his honor to kill Lönnrot, but the latter could never be intimidated. Lönnrot believed himself a pure reasoner, an Auguste Dupin, but there was something of the adventurer in him, and even a little of the gambler.

The first murder occurred in the Hôtel du Nord—that tall prism which dominates the estuary whose waters are the color of the desert. To that tower (which quite glaringly unites the hateful whiteness of a hospital, the numbered divisibility of a jail, and the general appearance of a bordello) there came on the third day of December the delegate from Podolsk to the Third Talmudic Congress, Doctor Marcel Yarmolinsky, a gray-bearded man with gray eyes. We shall never know whether the Hôtel du Nord pleased him; he accepted it with the ancient resignation which had allowed him to endure three years of war in the Carpathians and three thousand years of oppression and pogroms. He was given a room on Floor R, across from the suite which was occupied—not without splendor—by the Tetrarch of Galilee. Yarmolinsky supped, postponed until the following day an inspection of the unknown city, arranged in a *placard* his many books and few personal possessions, and before midnight extinguished his light. (Thus declared the Tetrarch's chauffeur who slept in the adjoining room.) On the fourth, at 11:03 A.M., the editor of the *Yidische Zaitung* put in a call to him; Doctor Yarmolinsky did not answer. He was found in his room, his face already a little dark, nearly nude beneath a large, anachronistic cape. He was lying not far from the door which opened on the hall; a deep knife wound had split his breast. A few hours later, in the same room amid journalists, photographers and policemen, Inspector Treviranus and Lönnrot were calmly discussing the problem.

"No need to look for a three-legged cat here," Treviranus was saying as he brandished an imperious cigar. "We all know that the Tetrarch of Galilee owns the finest sapphires in the world. Someone, intending to steal them, must have broken in here by mistake. Yarmolinsky got up; the robber had to kill him. How does it sound to you?"

"Possible, but not interesting," Lönnrot answered. "You'll reply that reality hasn't the least obligation to be interesting. And I'll answer you that reality may avoid that obligation but that hypotheses may not. In the hypothesis that you propose, chance intervenes copiously. Here we have a dead rabbi; I would prefer a purely rabbinical explanation, not the imaginary mischances of an imaginary robber."

Treviranus replied ill-humoredly:

"I'm not interested in rabbinical explanations. I am interested in capturing the man who stabbed this unknown person."

"Not so unknown," corrected Lönnrot. "Here are his complete works." He indicated in the wall-cupboard a row of tall books: a *Vindication of the Cabala; An Examination of the Philosophy of Robert Fludd;* a literal translation of the *Sepher Yezirah;* a *Biography of the Baal Shem;* a *History of the Hasidic Sect;* a monograph (in German) on the Tetragrammaton; another, on the divine nomenclature of the Pentateuch. The inspector regarded them with dread, almost with repulsion. Then he began to laugh.

"I'm a poor Christian," he said. "Carry off those musty volumes if you want; I don't have any time to waste on Jewish superstitions."

"Maybe the crime belongs to the history of Jewish superstitions," murmured Lönnrot.

"Like Christianity," the editor of the *Yidische Zaitung* ventured to add. He was myopic, an atheist and very shy.

No one answered him. One of the agents had found in the small typewriter a piece of paper on which was written the following unfinished sentence:

The first letter of the Name has been uttered

Lönnrot abstained from smiling. Suddenly become a bibliophile or Hebraist, he ordered a package made of the dead man's books and carried them off to his apartment. Indifferent to the police investigation, he dedicated himself to studying them. One large octavo volume revealed to him the teachings of Israel Baal Shem Tobh, founder of the sect of the Pious; another, the virtues and terrors of the Tetragrammaton, which is the unutterable name of God; another, the thesis that God has a secret name, in which is epitomized (as in the crys-

54

tal sphere which the Persians ascribe to Alexander of Macedonia) his ninth attribute, eternity—that is to say, the immediate knowledge of all things that will be, which are and which have been in the universe. Tradition numbers ninety-nine names of God; the Hebraists attribute that imperfect number to magical fear of even numbers; the Hasidim reason that that hiatus indicates a hundredth name—the Absolute Name.

From this erudition Lönnrot was distracted, a few days later, by the appearance of the editor of the *Yidische Zaitung*. The latter wanted to talk about the murder; Lönnrot preferred to discuss the diverse names of God; the journalist declared, in three columns, that the investigator, Erik Lönnrot, had dedicated himself to studying the names of God in order to come across the name of the murderer. Lönnrot, accustomed to the simplifications of journalism, did not become indignant. One of those enterprising shopkeepers who have discovered that any given man is resigned to buying any given book published a popular edition of the *History of the Hasidic Sect*.

The second murder occurred on the evening of the third of January, in the most deserted and empty corner of the capital's western suburbs. Towards dawn, one of the gendarmes who patrol those solitudes on horseback saw a man in a poncho, lying prone in the shadow of an old paint shop. The harsh features seemed to be masked in blood; a deep knife wound had split his breast. On the wall, across the yellow and red diamonds, were some words written in chalk. The gendarme spelled them out . . . That afternoon, Treviranus and Lönnrot headed for the remote scene of the crime. To the left and right of the automobile the city disintegrated; the firmament grew and houses were of less importance than a brick kiln or a poplar tree. They arrived at their miserable destination: an alley's end, with rose-colored walls which somehow seemed to reflect the extravagant sunset. The dead man had already been identified. He was Daniel Simon Azevedo, an individual of some fame in the old northern suburbs, who had risen from wagon driver to political tough, then degenerated to a thief and even an informer. (The singular style of his death seemed appropriate to them: Azevedo was the last representative of a generation of bandits who knew how to manipulate a dagger, but not a revolver.) The words in chalk were the following:

The second letter of the Name has been uttered

The third murder occurred on the night of the third of February. A little before one o'clock, the telephone in Inspector Treviranus' office rang. In avid secretiveness, a man with a guttural voice spoke; he said his name was Ginzberg (or Ginsburg) and that he was prepared to communicate, for reasonable remuneration, the events surrounding the two sacrifices of Azevedo and Yarmolinsky. A discordant sound of whistles and horns drowned out the informer's voice. Then, the connection was broken off. Without yet rejecting the possibility of a hoax (after all, it was carnival time), Treviranus found out that he had been called from the Liverpool House, a tavern on the rue de Toulon, that dingy street where side by side exist the cosmorama and the coffee shop, the bawdy house and the bible sellers. Treviranus spoke with the owner. The latter (Black Finnegan, an old Irish criminal who was immersed in, almost overcome by, respectability) told him that the last person to use the phone was a lodger, a certain Gryphius, who had just left with some friends. Treviranus went immediately to Liverpool House. The owner related the following. Eight days ago Gryphius had rented a room above the tavern. He was a sharp-featured man with a nebulous gray beard, and was shabbily dressed in black; Finnegan (who used the room for a purpose which Treviranus guessed) demanded a rent which was undoubtedly excessive; Gryphius paid the stipulated sum without hesitation. He almost never went out; he dined and lunched in his room; his face was scarcely known in the bar. On the night in question, he came downstairs to make a phone call from Finnegan's office. A closed cab stopped in front of the tavern. The driver didn't move from his seat; several patrons recalled that he was wearing a bear's mask. Two harlequins got out of the cab; they were of short stature and no one failed to observe that they were very drunk. With a tooting of horns, they burst into Finnegan's office; they embraced Gryphius, who appeared to recognize them but responded coldly; they exchanged a few words in Yiddish—he in a low, guttural voice, they in high-pitched, false voices—and then went up to the room. Within a quarter hour the three descended, very happy. Gryphius, staggering, seemed as drunk as the others. He walked—tall and dizzy—in the middle, between the masked harlequins. (One of the women at the bar remembered the yellow, red and green diamonds.) Twice he stumbled; twice he was caught and held by the harlequins. Moving off toward the inner harbor which enclosed a rectangular body of water, the three got into the cab and disappeared. From the footboard of the cab, the last of the harlequins scrawled an obscene figure and a sentence on one of the slates of the pier shed.

Treviranus saw the sentence. It was virtually predictable. It said:

The last of the letters of the Name has been uttered

Afterwards, he examined the small room of Gryphius-Ginzberg. On the floor there was a brusque star of blood, in the corners, traces of cigarettes of a Hungarian brand; in a cabinet, a book in Latin—*the Philologus Hebraeo-Graecus* (1739) of Leusden—with several manuscript notes. Treviranus looked it over with indignation and had Lönnrot located. The latter, without removing his hat, began to read while the inspector was interrogating the contradictory witnesses to the possible kidnapping. At four o'clock they left. Out on the twisted rue de Toulon, as they were treading on the dead serpentines of the dawn, Treviranus said:

"And what if all this business tonight were just a mock rehearsal?"

Erik Lönnrot smiled and, with all gravity, read a passage (which was underlined) from the thirty-third dissertation of the *Philologus: Dies Judacorum incipit ad solis occasu usque ad solis occasum diei sequentis.*

"This means," he added, "'The Hebrew day begins at sundown and lasts until the following sundown.'"

The inspector attempted an irony.

"Is that fact the most valuable one you've come across tonight?"

"No. Even more valuable was a word that Ginzberg used."

The afternoon papers did not overlook the periodic disappearances. *La Cruz de la Espada* contrasted them with the admirable discipline and order of the last Hermetical Congress; Ernst Palast, in *El Mártir,* criticized "the intolerable delays in this clandestine and frugal pogrom, which has taken three months to murder three Jews"; the *Yidische Zeitung* rejected the horrible hypothesis of an anti-Semitic plot, "even though many penetrating intellects admit no other solution to the triple mystery"; the most illustrious gunman of the south, Dandy Red Scharlach, swore that in his district similar crimes could never occur, and he accused Inspector Franz Treviranus of culpable negligence.

On the night of March first, the inspector received an

impressive-looking sealed envelope. He opened it; the envelope contained a letter signed "Baruch Spinoza" and a detailed plan of the city, obviously torn from a Baedeker. The letter prophesied that on the third of March there would not be a fourth murder, since the paint shop in the west, the tavern on the rue de Toulon and the Hôtel du Nord were "the perfect vertices of a mystic equilateral triangle"; the map demonstrated in red ink the regularity of the triangle. Treviranus read the *more geometrico* argument with resignation, and sent the letter and the map to Lönnrot—who, unquestionably, was deserving of such madnesses.

Erik Lönnrot studied them. The three locations were in fact equidistant. Symmetry in time (the third of December, the third of January, the third of February); symmetry in space as well . . . Suddenly, he felt as if he were on the point of solving the mystery. A set of calipers and a compass completed his quick intuition. He smiled, pronounced the word Tetragrammaton (of recent acquisition) and phoned the inspector. He said:

"Thank you for the equilateral triangle you sent me last night. It has enabled me to solve the problem. This Friday the criminals will be in jail, we may rest assured."

"Then they're not planning a fourth murder?"

"Precisely because they *are* planning a fourth murder we can rest assured."

Lönnrot hung up. One hour later he was traveling on one of the Southern Railway's trains, in the direction of the abandoned villa of Triste-le-Roy. To the south of the city of our story, flows a blind little river of muddy water, defamed by refuse and garbage. On the far side is an industrial suburb where, under the protection of a political boss from Barcelona, gunmen thrive. Lönnrot smiled at the thought that the most celebrated gunman of all—Red Scharlach—would have given a great deal to know of his clandestine visit. Azevedo had been an associate of Scharlach; Lönnrot considered the remote possibility that the fourth victim might be Scharlach himself. Then he rejected the idea . . . He had very nearly deciphered the problem; mere circumstances, reality (names, prison records, faces, judicial and penal proceedings) hardly interested him now. He wanted to travel a bit, he wanted to rest from three months of sedentary investigation. He reflected that the explanation of the murders was in an anonymous triangle and a dusty Greek word. The mystery appeared almost crystalline to him now; he was mortified to have dedicated a hundred days to it.

The train stopped at a silent loading station. Lönnrot got off. It was one of those deserted afternoons that seem like dawns. The air of the turbid, puddled plain was damp and cold. Lönnrot began walking along the countryside. He saw dogs, he saw a car on a siding, he saw the horizon, he saw a silver-colored horse drinking the crapulous water of a puddle. It was growing dark when he saw the rectangular belvedere of the villa of Triste-le-Roy, almost as tall as the black eucalypti which surrounded it. He thought that scarcely one dawning and one nightfall (an ancient splendor in the east and another in the west) separated him from the moment long desired by the seekers of the Name.

A rusty wrought-iron fence defined the irregular perimeter of the villa. The main gate was closed. Lönnrot, without much hope of getting in, circled the area. Once again before the insurmountable gate, he placed his hand between the bars almost mechanically and encountered the bolt. The creaking of the iron surprised him. With a laborious passivity the whole gate swung back.

Lönnrot advanced among the eucalypti treading on confused generations of rigid, broken leaves. Viewed from anear, the house of the villa of Triste-le-Roy abounded in pointless symmetries and in maniacal repetitions: to one Diana in a murky niche corresponded a second Diana in another niche; one balcony was reflected in another balcony; double stairways led to double balustrades. A two-faced Hermes projected a monstrous shadow. Lönnrot circled the house as he had the villa. He examined everything; beneath the level of the terrace he saw a narrow Venetian blind.

He pushed it; a few marble steps descended to a vault. Lönnrot, who had now perceived the architect's preferences, guessed that at the opposite wall there would be another stairway. He found it, ascended, raised his hands and opened the trap door.

A brilliant light led him to a window. He opened it: a yellow, rounded moon defined two silent fountains in the melancholy garden. Lönnrot explored the house. Through anterooms and galleries he passed to duplicate patios, and time after time to the same patio. He ascended the dusty stairs to circular antechambers; he was multiplied infinitely in opposing mirrors; he grew tired of opening or half-opening windows which revealed outside the same desolate garden from various heights and various angles; inside, only pieces of furniture wrapped in yellow dust sheets and chandeliers bound up in tarlatan. A bedroom detained him; in that bedroom, one single flower in a porcelain vase; at the first touch the ancient petals fell apart. On the second floor, on the top floor, the house seemed infinite and expanding. *The house is not this large,* he thought. *Other things are making it seem larger: the dim light, the symmetry, the mirrors, so many years, my unfamiliarity, the loneliness.*

By way of a spiral staircase he arrived at the oriel. The early evening moon shone through the diamonds of the window; they were yellow, red and green. An astonishing, dizzying recollection struck him.

Two men of short stature, robust and ferocious, threw themselves on him and disarmed him; another, very tall, saluted him gravely and said.

"You are very kind. You have saved us a night and a day."

It was Red Scharlach. The men handcuffed Lönnrot. The latter at length recovered his voice.

"Scharlach, are you looking for the Secret Name?"

Scharlach remained standing, indifferent. He had not participated in the brief struggle, and he scarcely extended his hand to receive Lönnrot's revolver. He spoke; Lönnrot noted in his voice a antigued triumph, a hatred the size of the universe, a sadness not less than that hatred.

"No," said scharlach. "I am seeking something more ephemeral and perishable, I am seeking Erik Lönnrot. Three years ago, in a gambling house on the rue de Toulon, you arrested my brother and had him sent to jail. My men slipped me away in a coupé from the gun battle with a policeman's bullet in my stomach. Nine days and nine nights I lay in agony in this desolate, symmetrical villa; fever was demolishing me, and the odious two-faced Janus who watches the twilights and the dawns lent horror to my dreams and to my waking. I came to abominate my body, I came to sense that two eyes, two hands, two lungs are as monstrous as two faces. An Irishman tried to convert me to the faith of Jesus; he repeated to me the phrase of the *goyim:* All roads lead to Rome. At night my delirium nurtured itself on that metaphor; I felt that the world was a labyrinth, from which it was impossible to flee, for all roads, though they pretend to lead to the north or south, actually lead to Rome, which was also the quadrilateral jail where my brother was dying and the villa of Triste-le-Roy. On those nights I swore by the God who sees with two faces and by all the gods of fever and of the mirrors to weave a labyrinth around the man who had imprisoned my brother. I have woven it and it is firm: the ingredients are a dead heresiologist, a compass, an eighteenth-century sect, a Greek word, a dagger, the diamonds of a paint shop.

"The first term of the sequence was given to me by chance. I had planned with a few colleagues—among them Daniel Azevedo—the robbery of the Tetrarch's sapphires. Azevedo betrayed us: he got drunk with the money that we had advanced him and he undertook the job a day early. He got lost in the vastness of the hotel; around two in the morning he stumbled into Yarmolinsky's room. The latter, harassed by insomnia, had started to write. He was working on some notes, apparently, for an article on the Name of God; he had already written the words: *The first letter of the Name has been uttered.* Azevedo warned him to be silent; Yarmolinsky reached out his hand for the bell which would awaken the hotel's forces; Azevedo countered with a single stab in the chest. It was almost a reflex action; half a century of violence had taught him that the easiest and surest thing is to kill . . . Ten days later I learned through the *Yidische Zaitung* that you were seeking in Yarmolinsky's writings the key to his death. I read the *History of the Hasidic Sect;* I learned that the reverent fear of uttering the Name of God had given rise to the doctrine that that Name is all powerful and recondite. I discovered that some Hasidim in search of that secret Name, had gone so far as to perform human sacrifices . . . I knew that you would make the conjecture that the Hasidim had sacrificed the rabbi; I set myself the task of justifying that conjecture.

"Marcel Yarmolinsky died on the night of December third; for the second 'sacrifice' I selected the night of January third. He died in the north; for the second 'sacrifice' a place in the west was suitable. Daniel Azevedo was the necessary victim. He deserved death; he was impulsive, a traitor; his apprehension could destroy the entire plan. One of us stabbed him; in order to link his corpse to the other one I wrote on the paint shop diamonds: *The second letter of the Name has been uttered.*

"The third murder was produced on the third of February. It was, as Treviranus guessed, a mere sham. I am Gryphius-Ginzberg-Ginsburg; I endured an interminable week (supplemented by a tenuous fake beard) in the perverse cubicle on the rue de Toulon, until my friends abducted me. From the footboard of the cab, one of them wrote on a post: *The last of the letters of the Name has been uttered.* That sentence revealed that the series of murders was *triple.* Thus the public understood it; I, nevertheless, interspersed repeated signs that would allow you, Erik Lönnrot, the reasoner, to understand that the series was quadruple. A portent in the north, others in the east and west, demand a fourth portent in the south; the Tetragrammaton—the name of God, JHVH—is made up of *four* letters; the harlequins and the paint shop sign suggested *four* points. In the manual of Leusden I underlined a certain passage: that passage manifests that Hebrews compute the day from sunset to sunset; that passage makes known that the deaths occurred on the *fourth* of each month. I sent the equilateral triangle to Treviranus. I foresaw that you would add the missing point. The point which would form a perfect rhomb, the point which fixes in advance where a punctual death awaits you. I have premeditated everything, Erik Lönnrot, in order to attract you to the solitudes of Triste-le-Roy."

Lönnrot avoided Scharlach's eyes. He looked at the trees and the sky subdivided into diamonds of turbid yellow, green and red. He felt faintly cold, and he felt, too, an impersonal—almost anonymous—sadness. It was already night; from the dusty garden came the futile cry of a bird. For the last time, Lönnrot considered the problem of the symmetrical and periodic deaths.

"In your labyrinth there are three lines too many," he said at last. "I know of one Greek labyrinth which is a single straight line. Along that line so many philosophers have lost themselves that a mere detective might well do so, too. Scharlach, when in some other incarnation you hunt me, pretend to commit (or do commit) a crime at A, then a second crime at B, eight kilometers from A, then a third crime at C, four kilometers from A and B, half-way between the two. Wait for me afterwards at D, two kilometers from A and C, again halfway between both. Kill me at D, as you are now going to kill me at Triste-le-Roy."

"The next time I kill you," replied Scharlach, "I promise you that labyrinth, consisting of a single line which is invisible and unceasing."

He moved back a few steps. Then, very carefully, he fired.

For Mandie Molina Vedia

Translated by Donald A. Yates

The Wall and the Books

He, whose long wall the wand'ring Tartar bounds . . .
Dunciad, II, 76

I read, some days past, that the man who ordered the erection of the almost infinite wall of China was that first Emperor, Shih Huang Ti, who also decreed that all books prior to him be burned. That these two vast operations—the five to six hundred leagues of stone opposing the barbarians, the rigorous abolition of history, that is, of the past—should originate in one person and be in some way his attributes inexplicably satisfied and, at the same time, disturbed me. To investigate the reasons for that emotion is the purpose of this note.

Historically speaking, there is no mystery in the two measures. A contemporary of the wars of Hannibal, Shih Huang Ti, king of Tsin, brought the Six Kingdoms under his rule and abolished the feudal system; he erected the wall, because walls were defenses; he burned the books, because his opposition invoked them to praise the emperors of olden times. Burning books and erecting fortifications is a common task of princes; the only thing singular in Shih Huang Ti was the scale on which he operated. Such is suggested by certain Sinologists, but I feel that the facts I have related are something more than an exaggeration or hyperbole of trivial dispositions. Walling in an orchard or a garden is ordinary, but not walling in an empire. Nor is it banal to pretend that the most traditional of races renounce the memory of its past, mythical or real. The Chinese had three thousand years of chronology (and during those years, the Yellow Emperor and Chuang Tsu and Confucius and Lao Tzu) when Shih Huang Ti ordered that history begin with him.

Shih Huang Ti had banished his mother for being a libertine; in his stern justice the orthodox saw nothing but an impiety; Shih Huang Ti, perhaps, wanted to obliterate the canonical books because they accused him; Shih Huang Ti, perhaps, tried to abolish the entire past in order to abolish one single memory: his mother's infamy. (Not in an unlike manner did a king of Judea have all male children killed in order to kill one.) This conjuecture is worthy of attention, but tells us nothing about the wall, the second part of the myth. Shih Huang Ti, according to the historians, forbade that death be mentioned and sought the elixir of immortality and secluded himself in a figurative palace containing as many rooms as there are days in the year; these facts suggest that the wall in space and the fire in time were magic barriers designed to halt death. All things long to persist in their being, Baruch Spinoza has written; perhaps the Emperor and his sorcerers believed that immortality is intrinsic and that decay cannot enter a closed orb. Perhaps the Emperor tried to recreate the beginning of time and called himself The First, so as to be really first, and called himself Huang Ti, so as to be in some way Huang Ti, the legendary emperor who invented writing and the compass. The latter, according to the *Book of Rites,* gave things their true name; in a parallel fashion, Shih Huang Ti boasted, in inscriptions which endure, that all things in his reign would have the name which was proper to them. He dreamt of founding an immortal dynasty; he ordered that his heirs be called Second Emperor, Third Emperor, Fourth Emperor, and so on to infinity . . . I have spoken of a magical purpose; it would also be fitting to suppose that erecting the wall and burning the books were not simultaneous acts. This (depending on the order we select) would give us the image of a king who began by destroying and then resigned himself to preserving, or that of a disillusioned king who destroyed what he had previously defended. Both conjectures are dramatic, but they lack, as far as I know, any basis in history. Herbert Allen Giles tells that those who hid books were branded with a red-hot iron and sentenced to labor until the day of their death on the construction of the outrageous wall. This information favors or tolerates another interpretation. Perhaps the wall was a metaphor, perhaps Shih Huang Ti sentenced those who worshiped the past to a task as immense, as gross and as useless as the past itself. Perhaps the wall was a challenge and Shih Huang Ti thought: "Men love the past and neither I nor my executioners can do anything against that love, but someday there will be a man who feels as I do and he will efface my memory and be my shadow and my mirror and not know it." Perhaps Shih Huang Ti walled in his empire because he knew that it was perishable and destroyed the books because he understood that they were sacred books, in other words, books that teach what the entire universe or the mind of every man teaches. Perhaps the burning of the libraries and the erection of the wall are operations which in some secret way cancel each other.

The tenacious wall which at this moment, and at all moments, casts its system of shadows over lands I shall never see, is the shadow of a Caesar who ordered the most reverent of nations to burn its past; it is plausible that this idea moves us in itself, aside from the conjectures it allows. (Its virtue may lie in the opposition of constructing and destroying on an enormous

scale.) Generalizing from the preceding case, we could infer that *all* forms have their virtue in themselves and not in any conjectural "content." This would concord with the thesis of Benedetto Croce; already Pater in 1877 had affirmed that all arts aspire to the state of music, which is pure form. Music, states of happiness, mythology, faces belabored by time, certain twilights and certain places try to tell us something, or have said something we should not have missed, or are about to say something; this imminence of a revelation which does not occur is, perhaps, the aesthetic phenomenon.

Translated by James E. Irby

Kafka and His Precursors

I once premeditated making a study of Kafka's precursors. At first I had considered him to be as singular as the phoenix of rhetorical praise; after frequenting his pages a bit, I came to think I could recognize his voice, or his practices, in texts from diverse literatures and periods. I shall record a few of these here, in chronological order.

The first is Zeno's paradox against movement. A moving object at A (declares Aristotle) cannot reach point B, because it must first cover half the distance between the two points, and before that, half of the half, and before that, half of the half of the half, and so on to infinity; the form of this illustrious problem is, exactly, that of *The Castle,* and the moving object and the arrow and Achilles are the first Kafkian characters in literature. In the second text which chance laid before me, the affinity is not one of form but one of tone. It is an apologue of Han Yu, a prose writer of the ninth century, and is reproduced in Margouliès' admirable *Anthologie raisonnée de la littérature chinoise* (1948). This is the paragraph, mysterious and calm, which I marked: "It is universally admitted that the unicorn is a supernatural being of good omen; such is declared in all the odes, annals, biographies of illustrious men and other texts whose authority is unquestionable. Even children and village women know that the unicorn constitutes a favorable presage. But this animal does not figure among the domestic beasts, it is not always easy to find, it does not lend itself to classification. It is not like the horse or the bull, the wolf or the deer. In such conditions, we could be face to face with a unicorn and not know for certain what it was. We know that such and such an animal with horns is a bull. But we do not know what the unicorn is like."[1]

The third text derives from a more easily predictable source: the writings of Kierkegaard. The spiritual affinity of both writers is something of which no one is ignorant; what has not yet been brought out, as far as I know, is the fact that Kierkegaard, like Kafka, wrote many religious parables on contemporary and bourgeois themes. Lowrie, in his *Kierkegaard* (Oxford University Press, 1938), transcribes two of these. One is the story of a counterfeiter who, under constant surveillance, counts banknotes in the Bank of England; in the same way, God would distrust Kierkegaard and have given him a task to perform, precisely because He knew that he was familiar with evil. The subject of the other parable is the North Pole expeditions. Danish ministers had declared from their pulpits that participation in these expeditions was beneficial to the soul's eternal well-being. They admitted, however, that it was difficult, and perhaps impossible, to reach the Pole and that not all men could undertake the adventure. Finally, they would announce that any trip—from Denmark to London, let us say, on the regularly scheduled steamer—was, properly considered, an expedition to the North Pole. The fourth of these prefigurations I have found is Browning's poem "Fears and Scruples," published in 1876. A man has, or

[1]Nonrecognition of the sacred animal and its opprobrious or accidental death at the hands of the people are traditional themes in Chinese literature. See the last chapter of Jung's *Psychologie und Alchemie* (Zürich, 1944), which contains two curious illustrations.

believes he has, a famous friend. He has never seen this friend and the fact is that the friend has so far never helped him, although tales are told of his most noble traits and authentic letters of his circulate about. Then someone places these traits in doubt and the handwriting experts declare that the letters are apocryphal. The man asks, in the last line: "And if this friend were . . . God?"

My notes also register two stories. One is from Léon Bloy's *Histoires désobligeantes* and relates the case of some people who possess all manner of globes, atlases, railroad guides and trunks, but who die without ever having managed to leave their home town. The other is entitled "Carcassonne" and is the work of Lord Dunsany. An invincible army of warriors leaves an infinite castle, conquers kingdoms and sees monsters and exhausts the deserts and the mountains, but they never reach Carcassonne, though once they glimpse it from afar. (This story is, as one can easily see, the strict reverse of the previous one; in the first, the city is never left; in the second, it is never reached.)

If I am not mistaken, the heterogeneous pieces I have enumerated resemble Kafka; if I am not mistaken, not all of them resemble each other. This second fact is the more significant. In each of these texts we find Kafka's idiosyncrasy to a greater or lesser degree, but if Kafka had never written a line, we would not perceive this quality; in other words, it would not exist. The poem "Fears and Scruples" by Browning foretells Kafka's work, but our reading of Kafka perceptibly sharpens and deflects our reading of the poem. Browning did not read it as we do now. In the critics' vocabulary, the word "precursor" is indispensable, but it should be cleansed of all connotation of polemics or rivalry. The fact is that every writer *creates* his own precursors. His work modifies our conception of the past, as it will modify the future.[1] In this correlation the identity or plurality of the men involved is unimportant. The early Kafka of *Betrachtung* is less a precursor of the Kafka of somber myths and atrocious institutions than is Browning or Lord Dunsany.

Translated by James E. Irby

---

[1]See T. S. Eliot: *Points of View* (1941), pp. 25–26.

Borges and I

The other one, the one called Borges, is the one things happen to. I walk through the streets of Buenos Aires and stop for a moment, perhaps mechanically now, to look at the arch of an entrance hall and the grillwork on the gate; I know of Borges from the mail and see his name on a list of professors or in a biographical dictionary. I like hourglasses, maps, eighteenth-century typography, the taste of coffee and the prose of Stevenson; he shares these preferences, but in a vain way that turns them into the attributes of an actor. It would be an exaggeration to say that ours is a hostile relationship; I live, let myself go on living, so that Borges may contrive his literature, and this literature justifies me. It is no effort for me to confess that he has achieved some valid pages, but those pages cannot save me, perhaps because what is good belongs to no one, not even to him, but rather to the language and to tradition. Besides, I am destined to perish, definitively, and only some instant of myself can survive in him. Little by little, I am giving over everything to him, though I am quite aware of his perverse custom of falsifying and magnifying things. Spinoza knew that all things long to persist in their being; the stone eternally wants to be a stone and the tiger a tiger. I shall remain in Borges, not myself (if it is true that I am someone), but I recognize myself less in his books than in many others or in the laborious strumming of a guitar. Years ago I tried to free myself from him and went from the mythologies of the suburbs to the games with time and infinity, but those games belong to Borges now and I shall have to imagine other things. Thus my life is a flight and I lose everything and everything belongs to oblivion, or to him.

I do not know which of us has written this page.

Translated by James E. Irby

Everything and Nothing

There was no one in him: behind his face (which even through the bad paintings of those times resembles no other) and his words, which were copious, fantastic and stormy, there was only a bit of coldness, a dream dreamt by no one. At first he thought that all people were like him, but the astonishment of a friend to whom he had begun to speak of this emptiness showed him his error and made him feel always that an individual should not differ in outward appearance. Once he thought that in books he would find a cure for his ill and thus he learned the small Latin and less Greek a contemporary would speak of; later he considered that what he sought might well be found in an element rite of humanity, and let himself be initiated by Anne Hathaway one long June afternoon. At the age of twenty-odd years he went to London. Instinctively he had already become proficient in the habit of simulating that he was someone, so that others would not discover his condition as no one; in London he found the profession to which he was predestined, that of the actor, who on a stage plays at being another before a gathering of people who play at taking him for that other person. His histrionic tasks brought him a singular satisfaction, perhaps the first he had ever known; but once the last verse had been acclaimed and the last dead man withdrawn from the stage, the hated flavor of unreality returned to him. He ceased to be Ferrex or

Tamerlane and became no one again. Thus hounded, he took to imagining other heroes and other tragic fables. And so, while his flesh fulfilled its destiny as flesh in the taverns and brothels of London, the soul that inhabited him was Caesar, who disregards the augur's admonition, and Juliet, who abhors the lark, and Macbeth, who converses on the plain with the witches who are also Fates. No one has ever been so many men as this man, who like the Egyptian Proteus could exhaust all the guises of reality. At times he would leave a confession hidden away in some corner of his work, certain that it would not be deciphered; Richard affirms that in his person he plays the part of many and Iago claims with curious words "I am not what I am." The fundamental identity of existing, dreaming and acting inspired famous passages of his.

For twenty years he persisted in that controlled hallucination, but one morning he was suddenly gripped by the tedium and the terror of being so many kings who die by the sword and so many suffering lovers who converge, diverge and melodiously expire. That very day he arranged to sell his theater. Within a week he had returned to his native village, where he recovered the trees and rivers of his childhood and did not relate them to the others his muse had celebrated, illustrious with mythological allusions and Latin terms. He had to be someone; he was a retired impresario who had made his fortune and concerned himself with loans, lawsuits and petty usury. It was in this character that he dictated the arid will and testament known to us, from which he deliberately excluded all traces of pathos or literature. His friends from London would visit his retreat and for them he would take up again his role as poet.

History adds that before or after dying he found himself in the presence of God and told Him: "I who have been so many men in vain want to be one and myself." The voice of the Lord

77

answered from a whirlwind: "Neither am I anyone; I have dreamt the world as you dreamt your work, my Shakespeare, and among the forms in my dream are you, who like myself are many and no one."

Translated by James E. Irby

Nightmares

Dreams are the genus; nightmares the species. I will speak first of dreams, and then of nightmares.

Lately I've been reading psychology books, and I have felt singularly defrauded. All of them discuss the mechanisms of dreams or the subjects of dreams, but they do not mention, as I had hoped, that which is so astonishing, so strange—the fact of dreaming.

Thus, in a psychology book I admire greatly, *The Mind of Man,* Gustav Spiller states that dreams correspond to the lowest plane of mental activity—I would maintain that, at least for me, this is an error—and he speaks of the incoherence, the disconnectedness, of the fables of dreams. I would like to recall Paul Groussac and his fine essay, "Among Dreams." in *The Intellectual Voyage.* Groussac writes that it is astonishing that each morning we wake up sane—that is, relatively sane—after having passed through that zone of shades, those labyrinths of dreams.

The study of dreams is particularly difficult, for we cannot examine dreams directly, we can only speak of the memory of dreams. And it is possible that the memory of dreams does not correspond exactly to the dreams themselves. A great writer of the eighteenth century, Sir Thomas Browne, believed that our memory of dreams is more impoverished than the splendor of reality. Others, in turn, believe that we improve our dreams. If

we think of the dream as a work of fiction—and I think it is—
it may be that we continue to spin tales when we wake and
later when we recount them.

I want to recall that great book by Boethius, *De consolatione
philosophiae,* which Dante read and reread, as he read and
reread all of the literature of the Middle Ages. Boethius, who
has been called "the last Roman," Boethius the senator imagined a spectator at a horse race.

The spectator is in the hippodrome, and he sees, from his
box, the horses at the starting gate, all the vicissitudes of the
race itself, and the arrival of one of the horses at the finishing
line. He sees it all in succession. Boethius then imagines another spectator. This other spectator is the spectator of the
spectator of the race; he is, let us say, God. God sees the whole
race; he sees in a single eternal instant the start, the race, the
finish. He sees everything in a single glance; and in the same
way he sees all of history. Thus Boethius bridges the concepts
of free will and of Providence. Just as the spectator sees the
race (albeit sequentially) but does not influence it, so God sees
the whole race from cradle to tomb. He does not influence
what we do. We act by our own free will, but God knows—
God knows at this very moment—our final destiny. God sees
all of history, what unfolds as history, in a single splendid
dizzying instant that is eternity.

I think now of that book, *An Experiment with Time*—I
know no title more interesting—by J. W. Dunne, an English
writer of this century. I do not agree with his theory, but it is
so beautiful it's worth recalling. In the book he imagines that
each one of us possesses a kind of modest personal eternity:
one we possess each night. Tonight we will sleep, and
tonight, Wednesday night, we will dream. And we will dream
of Wednesday and of the next day, Thursday, and perhaps of
Friday, and perhaps of Tuesday . . . Each man is given, in

dreams, a little personal eternity which allows him to see the recent past and the near future.

All of this the dreamer sees in a single glance, in the same way that God, from His vast eternity, sees the whole cosmic process. And what happens when we wake? What happens is that, as we are accustomed to a sequential life, we give a narrative structure to our dream, though our dream has been multiple and simultaneous.

Let us look at a very simple example. Suppose I dream of a man, simply the image of a man—I'm using a very poor dream—and then, immediately after, I dream the image of a tree. Waking, I can give this dream a complexity it does not have: I can think I have dreamed that a man has been changed into a tree, that he was a tree. Modifying the facts, I spin a tale.

We don't know exactly what happens in dreams. It is not impossible that during dreams, we are in heaven, we are in hell. Perhaps we are someone, the someone whom Shakespeare called "the thing I am"; perhaps we are ourselves, perhaps we are God. All of this we forget at waking. We can only examine the memory of a dream, the poor memory.

I have read Frazer—a supremely talented writer, but also an extremely credulous one, as it seems he believed everything reported by the various travelers. According to Frazer, savages do not distinguish between waking and dreaming. For them, dreams are episodes of the waking life. Thus, according to Frazer, or according to the travelers he read, a savage dreams he goes into the forest and kills a lion. When he wakes, he thinks his soul has abandoned his body and has killed a lion in his dreams. Or, if we want to complicate things a little, we may suppose that he has killed the dream of a lion. All of this is possible, and this idea of the savages coincides with that of children, who also cannot distinguish between waking and dream.

81

I will recall a personal memory. A nephew of mine—he was about five or six at the time—used to tell me his dreams each morning. One day, as he was sitting on the floor, I asked him what he had dreamed. Patiently, knowing that I had this *hobby,* he told me: "Last night I dreamed that I was lost in the forest. I was scared, but I came to a clearing, and there was a white house, made of wood, with a staircase that turned around, with steps with runners, and then a door, and out of this door you came out." He suddenly stopped: "But what were *you* doing in that house?"

Everything, waking and dream, occurred for him on a single plane. This brings us to another, similar but contrary, hypothesis: that of the mystics and the metaphysicians.

For the savage and for the child, dreams are episodes of the waking life; for poets and mystics, it is not impossible for all of the waking life to be a dream. This was said, in a dry and laconic fashion, by Calderón: "Life is a dream." It was said, with an image, by Shakespeare: "We are such stuff as dreams are made on." And splendidly by the Austrian poet Walter von Vogelweide, who asked, "*Ist mein Leben geträumt oder ist es wahr?*"—have I dreamed my life or is it real? I am not sure. It takes us certainly to solipsism, to the suspicion that there is only one dreamer and that dreamer is every one of us. That dreamer—let us imagine that I am he—is, at this very moment, dreaming you. He is dreaming this room and this lecture. There is only one dreamer, and that dreamer dreams all of the cosmic process, dreams all of the world's history, dreams everything, including your childhood and your adolescence. All this could not have happened; at this moment it begins to exist. He begins to dream and is each one of us—not *us,* but *each one.* At this moment I am dreaming that I am giving a lecture on the Calle Charcas, that I am looking for things to say (and perhaps not finding them); I am dreaming you. But it is not true. Each one of you is dreaming me and the others.

We have these two ideas: the belief that dreams are part of waking, and the other, the splendid one, the belief of the poets: that all of waking is a dream. There is no difference between the two. It takes us back to Groussac's article: we may be awake, we may be asleep and dreaming, but our mental activity is the same.

There is a passage in the *Odyssey* where it speaks of two gates, one of horn and one of ivory. Through the ivory gate false dreams pass to men, and through the gate of horn go the true and prophetic dreams. And there is a passage in the *Aeneid,* in the sixth book, which has provoked innumerable commentaries. Aeneas descends to the Elysian Fields, beyond the Pillars of Hercules. He speaks with the shades of Achilles and Tiresias; he sees the shade of his mother, he wants to embrace her but cannot because she is made of shadow; and he sees, moreover, the future greatness of the city he will found. He sees Romulus and Remus, a field, and then in that field the future Roman Forum, the future grandeur of Rome, the greatness of Augustus; he sees the whole imperial grandeur. And after having seen all of this, after having talked to its contemporaries (who, for Aeneas, are future people), he returns to the world of the living. What then occurs is quite curious and has never been well explained, except by one anonymous commentator who I believe offered the truth. Aeneas returns through the gate of ivory and not through the gate of horn. Why? The anonymous commentator tells us: because we are not in reality. For Virgil, the real world was possibly the Platonic world, the world of the archetypes. Aeneas passes through the gates of ivory because he enters the world of dreams—that is to say, what we call waking.

Well, all of this may well be.

Now we come to the species, to nightmare. It may be useful to recall the names of nightmare.

The Spanish name, *pesadilla,* is too cheerful: the diminutive -*illa* makes it lack force. In other languages the names are more powerful. In Greek the word is *ephialtes:* Ephialtes is the demon who inspires nightmares. In Latin we have *incubus.* The incubus is the demon who crushes the sleeper, causing the nightmare. In German we have a very curious word, *Alp,* which has come to mean both the elf and the torment brought by elf—the same idea of a demon who inspires nightmares. There is a painting that De Quincey, one of literature's great dreamers of nightmares, saw. It is a painting by Fuseli or Füssli (which was his actual name; he was a Swiss painter of the eighteenth century) called *The Nightmare.* A girl is sleeping. She wakes and is terrified because she sees lying on her belly a monster that is small, black, and malign. This monster is the nightmare. When Fuseli painted this picture he was thinking of the word *Alp,* of the elf's torments.

We come now to the wisest and most ambiguous word, the English *nightmare,* which means the mare of the night. This was how Shakespeare understood it. There is a line of his that says, "I met the night mare." Clearly he saw it as a mare. And there is another line where he says, deliberately, "the night-mare and her nine foals."

But according to the etymologists the root is different. The root is *niht mare* or *niht maere,* the demon of the night. Dr. Johnson, in his famous dictionary, says that this corresponds to Nordic mythology—Saxon mythology we would say—which saw nightmares as the products of demons. This would make it a play on, or translation of, the Greek *ephialtes* or the Latin *incubus.*

There is another interpretation that may help us, one that

relates *nightmare* to the German word *Märchen. Märchen* means fable, fairy tale, fiction. Nightmare, then, would be the fiction of the night. Whatever the case, the fact of conceiving of nightmare as a mare of the night—there is something terrifying in a mare of the night—was a boon for Victor Hugo. Hugo mastered English and wrote an unjustly forgotten book on Shakespeare. In one of his poems, I think in *Les contemplations,* he speaks of *"le cheval noir de la nuit,"* the black horse of night. No doubt he was thinking of the English word *nightmare.*

We also have the French word, *cauchemar,* which is probably linked to *nightmare.* In all of these words there is an idea of demonic origin, the idea of a demon who causes the nightmare. I believe it does not derive simply from a superstition. I believe that there is—and I speak with complete honesty and sincerity—something true in this idea.

Let us enter into the nightmare, into nightmares. Mine are always the same. I have two nightmares which often become confused with one another. I have the nightmare of the labyrinth, which comes, in part, from a steel engraving I saw in a French book when I was a child. In this engraving were the Seven Wonders of the World, among them the labyrinth of Crete. The labyrinth was a great amphitheater, a very high amphitheater (and this was apparent because it was higher than the cypresses and the men outside it). In this closed structure—ominously closed—there were cracks. I believed when I was a child (or I now believe I believed) that if one had a magnifying glass powerful enough, one could look through the cracks and see the Minotaur in the terrible center of the labyrinth.

My other nightmare is that of the mirror. The two are not distinct, as it only takes two facing mirrors to construct a labyrinth. I remember seeing, in the house of Dora de Alvear in the Belgrano district, a circular room whose walls and doors were mirrored, so that whoever entered the room found himself at the center of a truly infinite labyrinth.

I always dream of labyrinths or of mirrors. In the dream of the mirror another vision appears, another terror of my nights, and that is the idea of the mask. Masks have always scared me. No doubt I felt in my childhood that someone who was wearing a mask was hiding something horrible. These are my most terrible nightmares: I see myself reflected in a mirror, but the reflection is wearing a mask. I am afraid to pull the mask off, afraid to see my real face, which I imagine to be hideous. There may be leprosy or evil or something more terrible than anything I am capable of imagining.

A curious feature of my nightmares—I don't know if you share this with me—is that they have a precise topography. I, for example, always dream of certain corners in Buenos Aires. I'm on the corner of Laprida and Arenales, or the one at Balcarce and Chile. I know exactly where I am, and I know that I must head toward some far-off place. These places in my dreams have a precise topography, but they are completely different. They may be mountain paths or swamps or jungles, it doesn't matter: I know that I am on a certain corner in Buenos Aires. I try to find my way.

Although one might wish otherwise, in dreams what is important is not the images. What matters, as Coleridge said, is the impression produced by the dream. The images are minor; they are effects.

Let us look at a line by Petronius, quoted by Addison. (I am deliberately citing poets, who are particularly illuminating.) He says that, "The soul, without the body, plays." Góngora, in a sonnet, expresses with precision the idea that dreams and nightmares are, above all, fictions; they are literary creations:

El sueño, autor de representaciones,
en su teatro sobre el viento armado
sombras suele vestir de bulto bello.

[The dream, author of representations, /in its
theater above the armored wind /dresses
shadows in beautiful bulk.]

The dream is a representation. Addison reinterpreted the
idea according to eighteenth-century principles in an excellent
article published in *The Spectator.*

I have cited Sir Thomas Browne. He says that dreams give
us an idea of the excellence of the soul, seeing the soul free of
the body and engaged in play and dreaming. He thinks that
the soul enjoys its freedom. And Addison says effectively that
the soul, when it is free of the shackles of the body, imagines,
and is able to imagine with a freedom it does not have in waking. He adds that of all the operations of the soul—of the
mind we would say, now that we don't use the word *soul*—the
most difficult is invention. Yet in dreams we invent so rapidly
that we confuse our thoughts with our inventions. We dream
we are reading a book, and the truth is we have invented every
word in the book. But we don't realize it, and we take it as
strange. I have noted in many dreams this anticipatory
process, which prepares us for the things to come.

I remember a certain nightmare I had. It took place, I
know, on the Calle Serrano, I think at the corner of Serrano
and Soler. It did not look like Serrano and Soler—the land-
scape was quite different—but I *knew* that I was on the old
Calle Serrano in the Palermo district. I met a friend, a friend I
do not know; I saw him, and he was much changed. I had
never seen his face before, but I knew his face could not be like
that. He was much changed, and very sad. His face was

marked by troubles, by illness, perhaps by guilt. He had his right hand inside his jacket. I couldn't see his hand, which he kept hidden over his heart. I embraced him and felt that I had to help him. "But, my poor Fulano, what has happened? How changed you are!" "Yes," he answered, "I am much changed." Slowly, he withdrew his hand. I could see that it was the claw of a bird.

The strange thing is that from the beginning the man had his hand hidden. Without knowing it, I had paved the way for that invention: that the man had the claw of a bird and that I would see the terrible change, the terrible misfortune, that he was turning into a bird. It also happens in dreams that are not nightmares: they ask us something, and we don't know how to answer; they give us the answer, and we are astonished. The answer may be absurd, but in the dream it is exactly right. Everything has been prepared. I have come to the conclusion, though it may not be scientific, that dreams are the most ancient aesthetic activity.

We know that animals dream. There are Latin verses that speak of the greyhound barking at the hare it chases in dreams. What is curious is the dramatic order of dreams. Addison observed that in the dream we are the theater, the audience, the actors, the plot, the dialogue we hear. We make up everything unconsciously, and everything has a vivacity it does not have in reality. There are people who have weak dreams, vague ones——or, at least, so they tell me. Mine are quite vivid.

Let us return to Coleridge. He says it doesn't matter what we dream, that the dream searches for explanations. He gives an example: a lion suddenly appears in this room, and we all are afraid; the fear has been caused by the image of the lion. But in dreams the reverse can occur. We feel oppressed, and then search for an explanation. I, absurdly but vividly, dream that a sphinx has lain down next to me. The sphinx is not the cause of my fear, it is an explanation of my feeling of oppression. Coleridge adds that people who have been frightened by imaginary ghosts have gone mad. On the other hand, a person who dreams a ghost can wake up and, within a few seconds, regain his composure.

I have had—and I still have—many nightmares. The most terrible, the one that struck me as the most terrible, I used in a sonnet. It went like this: I was in my room; it was dawn (possibly that was the time of the dream). At the foot of my bed was a king, a very ancient king, and I knew in the dream that he was the King of the North, of Norway. He did not look at me; his blind stare was fixed on the ceiling. I felt the terror of his presence. I saw the king, I saw his sword, I saw his dog. Then I woke. But I continued to see the king for a while, because he had made such a strong impression on me. Retold, my dream is nothing; dreamt, it was terrible.

I want to mention a nightmare my friend Susana Bombal recently told me. She dreamed she was in a vaulted room, the top of which was in darkness. From the darkness dropped a black, unraveling piece of cloth. In her hand she awkwardly held a giant pair of scissors. She had to cut the loose threads that hung from the cloth, and they were endless. She kept snipping but she knew she would never finish. And she had the sensation of horror that is the nightmare; for the nightmare is, above all, the sensation of horror.

I have recounted two actual nightmares, and now I will describe two nightmares from literature, which possibly were also real. The first is the *nobile castello* which Dante imagined in the *Inferno*. Dante tells how, guided by Virgil, he reaches the first circle and sees that Virgil has turned pale. He thinks: if Virgil turns pale entering Hell, which is his eternal domain, why do I not feel afraid? He tells this to Virgil, who is terrified. But Virgil says: "I will go first." They go in despair, for they hear around them infinite sighs—not the sighs of physical pain, but the sighs of something more grave.

They come to a noble castle, to the *nobile castello*. It is encircled by seven walls that may be the seven liberal arts of the *trivium* and the *quadrivium* or the seven virtues; it doesn't matter. He speaks of a river that disappears and of a fresh meadow that also disappears. When they reach the meadow, they see that it is enameled, that it is not a living thing. Four shades approach them: the shades of the four great poets of Antiquity. There is Homer, sword in hand; Ovid, Lucan, and Horace. Virgil tells him to greet Homer, whom Dante revered and never read. He tells him, *"Onorate l'altissimo poeta."* Homer comes forward, sword in hand, and admits Dante as the sixth of the company. Dante, who had still not written the *Commedia* because he was writing it at that moment, knows himself to be capable of writing it.

They then discuss things which Dante does not bother to repeat. We may wonder at the Florentine's modesty, but I think there is a deeper reason. He speaks of those who inhabit the noble castle: there are the great shades of the pagans, and of the Moslems too. They all speak slowly and softly, they have faces of great authority, but they are deprived of God. There is the absence of God. They know they are condemned to that eternal castle, to that castle that is eternal and honorable, but terrible.

There is Aristotle, master of those who know. There are the pre-Socratic philosophers; there is Plato and, alone and apart, the great sultan Saladin. There are all the great pagans who could not be saved because they were never baptized. They could not be saved by Christ, of whom Virgil speaks but cannot name in Hell—he calls him the Mighty One. We may think that Dante had not yet discovered his dramatic talent, he did not yet know that he could make those figures speak.

We may lament that Dante does not repeat the great words, no doubt dignified, that Homer, that grand shade, told him, sword in hand. But we may also feel that Dante understood it was better for all to be silent in that terrible castle. Dante merely names them: Seneca, Plato, Aristotle, Saladin, Averroës. He names them, and we don't hear a single word. It's better that way.

I would say, thinking of the *Inferno,* that Hell is not a nightmare; it is simply a torture chamber. Atrocious things take place there, but it does not have the atmosphere of a nightmare that there is in the "noble castle." This is what Dante gives us, perhaps for the first time in literature.

There is another example, one that was praised by De Quincey. It is in the fifth book of Wordsworth's *Prelude.* Wordworth says that he was preoccupied by the fact that art and science were at the mercy of some cataclysm. (Such a preoccupation was rare at the beginning of the nineteenth century. Today, of course, we think that all of the works of humanity, and humanity itself, could be destroyed in a moment by the atomic bomb.) Well . . . Wordsworth is talking with a friend, and he expresses his horror at the thought that the great works of mankind, the sciences and the arts, could be destroyed. The friend confesses that he too has felt such fears. And Wordsworth says: I have dreamed it . . .

And then comes a dream which seems to me the perfect nightmare, for it contains all the elements of nightmare: episodes of physical ill-being, of persecution, and the element of horror, of the supernatural. Wordsworth tells us that he was in a rocky cave by the sea. It was noon, and he was reading *Don Quixote,* one of his favorite books, "the famous history of the errant knight recorded by Cervantes." He put down the book and began to think about the end of science and art, and then the hour came. The powerful hour of noon, a hot summer noon. "Sleep seized me," he recalls, "and I passed into a dream."

He falls asleep in the cave, facing the sea, amid the golden sands of the beach. In his dream he is also surrounded by sand, a Sahara of black sand. There is no water, there is no sea. He is in the middle of a desert—in the desert one is always in the middle—and he is horrified at the thought of trying to escape. Suddenly he sees there is someone next to him. It is, oddly enough, an Arab of the Bedouin tribes, mounted on a camel and with a lance in his right hand. Under his left arm he has a stone, and in his hand he holds a shell. The Arab tells him that his mission is to save the arts and sciences. He brings the shell to the poet's ear; the shell is of an extraordinary beauty. Wordsworth tells us he hears a prophecy "in an unknown tongue which yet I understood": a sort of tender ode, prophesying that the earth was on the verge of being destroyed by a flood sent by the wrath of God. The Arab tells him that it is true, the flood is coming, but that he has a mission: to save the arts and sciences. He shows him the stone. And the stone is, curiously, Euclid's *Elements,* while remaining a stone. Then he brings the shell closer, and the shell too is a book; it is what had spoken those terrible things. The shell is, moreover, all the poetry of the world, including—why not?—the poem by Wordsworth. The Bedouin tells him that he must save these two things, the stone and the shell, both of them books. He turns around, and there is a moment in which Wordsworth sees that the face of the Bedouin has changed, that it is full of horror. He too turns around, and he sees a great light, a light that has now flooded the middle of the desert. It is the waters of the flood that will destroy the earth. The Bedouin goes off, and Wordsworth sees that the Bedouin is also Don Quixote and that the camel is also Rosinante and that, in the same way that the stone was a book and the shell a book, so the Bedouin is Don Quixote and is neither of the two and is both at once. This duality corresponds to the horror of the dream. Wordsworth, at that moment, wakes with a cry of terror, for the waters have engulfed him.

I think that this nightmare is one of the most beautiful in literature.

We may draw two conclusions, at least tonight; later we can change our minds. The first is that dreams are an aesthetic work, perhaps the most ancient aesthetic expression. They take a strangely dramatic form. We are, as Addison said, the theater, the spectators, the actors, the story. The second refers to the horror of nightmares. Our waking life abounds in terrible moments; we all know that there are moments in which reality overwhelms us. A loved one has died, a loved one has left us; such are the causes of sadness, of despair . . . Nevertheless, these do not pertain to nightmares. The nightmare has a particular horror, and that horror may be expressed by any story. It may be expressed by Wordsworth's Bedouin who is also Don Quixote, by scissors and threads, by my dream of the king, by the famous nightmares of Poe. But there is something: it is the *flavor* of the nightmare. In the treatises I have consulted they do not speak of this horror.

We also have the possibility of a theological interpretation, one that would be in accord with etymology. Take any of the words: the Latin *incubus,* the Saxon *nightmare,* the German *Alp.* All of them suggest something supernatural. Well, what if nightmares were strictly supernatural? What if nightmares were cries from hell? What if nightmares literally took place in hell? Why not? Everything is so strange that even this is possible.

Translated by Eliot Weinberger

Blindness

In the course of the many lectures—too many lectures—I have given, I've observed that people tend to prefer the personal to the general, the concrete to the abstract. I will begin, then, by referring to my own modest blindness. Modest, because it is total blindness in one eye, but only partial in the other. I can still make out certain colors; I can still see blue and green. And yellow, in particular, has remained faithful to me. I remember when I was young I used to linger in front of certain cages in the Palermo zoo: the cages of the tigers and leopards. I lingered before the tiger's gold and black. Yellow is still with me, even now. I have written a poem entitled "The Gold of the Tigers," in which I refer to this friendship.

People generally imagine the blind as enclosed in a black world. There is, for example, Shakespeare's line: "Looking on darkness which the blind do see." If we understand *darkness* as *blackness,* then Shakespeare is wrong.

One of the colors that the blind—or at least this blind man—do *not* see is black; another is red. *Le rouge et le noir* are the colors denied us. I, who was accustomed to sleeping in total darkness, was bothered for a long time at having to sleep in this world of mist, in the greenish or bluish mist, vaguely luminous, which is the world of the blind. I wanted to lie down in darkness. The world of the blind is not the night that people imagine. (I should say that I am speaking for myself, and for my father and my grandmother, who both died blind—blind, laughing, and brave, as I also hope to die. They inherited many things—blindness, for example—but one does not inherit courage. I know that they were brave.)

The blind live in a world that is inconvenient, an undefined world from which certain colors emerge: for me, yellow, blue (except that the blue may be green), and green (except that the green may be blue). White had disappeared, or is confused with gray. As for red, it has vanished completely. But I hope some day—I am following a treatment—to improve and to be able to see that great color, that color which shines in poetry, and which has so many beautiful names in many languages. Think of *scharlach* in German, *scarlet* in English, *escarlata* in Spanish, *écarlate* in French. Words that are worthy of that great color. In contrast, *amarillo,* yellow, sounds weak in Spanish, in English it seems more like yellow. I think that in Old Spanish it was *amariello.*

I live in that world of colors, and if I speak of my own modest blindness, I do so, first, because it is not that perfect blindness which people imagine, and second, because it deals with me. My case is not especially dramatic. What is dramatic are those who suddenly lose their sight. In my case, that slow nightfall, that slow loss of sight, began when I began to see. It has continued since 1899 without dramatic moments, a slow nightfall that has lasted more than three quarters of a century. In 1955 the pathetic moment came when I knew I had lost my sight, my reader's and writer's sight.

In my life I have received many unmerited honors, but there is one which has made me happier than all the others: the directorship of the National Library. For reasons more political than literary, I was appointed by the Aramburu government.

I was named director of the library, and I returned to that

building of which I had so many memories, on the Calle México in Monserrat, in the South of the city. I had never dreamed of the possibility of being director of the library. I had memories of another kind. I would go there with my father, at night. My father, a professor of psychology, would ask for some book by Bergson or William James, who were his favorite writers, or perhaps by Gustav Spiller. I, too timid to ask for a book, would look through some volume of the *Encyclopedia Britannica* or the German encyclopedias of Brockhaus or of Meyer. I would take a volume at random from the shelf and read. I remember one night when I was particularly rewarded, for I read three articles: on the Druids, the Druses, and Dryden—a gift of the letters *dr.* Other nights I was less fortunate.

I knew that Paul Groussac was in the building. I could have met him personally, but I was then quite shy; almost as shy as I am now. At the time, I believed that shyness was very important, but now I know that shyness is one of the evils one must try to overcome, that in reality to be shy doesn't matter—it is like so many other things to which one gives an exaggerated importance.

I received the nomination at the end of 1955. I was in charge of, I was told, a million books. Later I found out it was nine hundred thousand—a number that's more than enough. (And perhaps nine hundred thousand seems more than a million.)

Little by little I came to realize the strange irony of events. I had always imagined Paradise as a kind of library. Others think of a garden or of a palace. There I was, the center, in a way, of nine hundred thousand books in various languages, but I found I could barely make out the title pages and the spines. I wrote the "Poem of the Gifts," which begins:

No one should read self-pity or reproach
into this statement of the majesty
of God; who with such splendid irony
granted me books and blindness at one touch.
[tr. Alastair Reid]

Those two gifts contradicted each other: the countless books and the night, the inability to read them.

I imagined the author of that poem to be Groussac, for Groussac was also the director of the library and also blind. Groussac was more courageous than I: he kept his silence. But I knew that there had certainly been moments when our lives had coincided, since we both had become blind and we both loved books. He honored literature with books far superior to mine. But we were both men of letters, and we both passed through the library of forbidden books—one might say, for our darkened eyes, of blank books, books without letters. I wrote of the irony of God, and in the end I asked myself which of us had written that poem of a plural I and a single shadow.

At the time I did not know that there had been another director of the library who was blind, José Mármol. Here appears the number three, which seals everything. Two is a mere coincidence; three a confirmation. A confirmation of a ternary order, a divine or theological confirmation.

Mármol was director of the library when it was on the Calle Venezuela. These days it is usual to speak badly of Mármol, or not to mention him at all. But we must remember that when we speak of the time of Rosas, we do not think of the admirable book by Ramos Mejía, *Rosas y su tiempo* ("*Rosas and his time*"), but of the era as it is described in Mármol's wonderfully gossipy novel, *La Amalia*. To bequeath the image of an age or of a country is no small glory.

We have, then, three people who shared the same fate. And, for me, the joy of returning to the Monserrat section, in the South. For everyone in Buenos Aires, the South is, in a mysterious way, the secret center of the city. Not the other, somewhat ostentatious center we show to tourists—in those days there was not that bit of public relations called the Barrio de San Telmo. But the South has come to be the modest secret center of Buenos Aires.

When I think of Buenos Aires, I think of the Buenos Aires I knew as a child: the low houses, the patios, the porches, the cisterns with turtles in them, the grated windows. That Buenos Aires was all of Buenos Aires. Now only the southern section has been preserved. I felt that I had returned to the neighborhood of my elders.

There were the books, but I had to ask my friends the names of them. I remembered a sentence from Rudolf Steiner, in his books on anthroposophy, which was the name he gave to his theosophy. He said that when something ends, we must think that something begins. His advice is salutory, but the execution is difficult, for we only know what we have lost, not what we will gain. We have a very precise image—an image at times shameless—of what we have lost, but we are ignorant of what may follow or replace it.

I made a decision. I said to myself: since I have lost the beloved world of appearances, I must create something else. At the time I was a professor of English at the University. What could I do to teach that almost infinite literature, that literature which exceeds the life of a man, and even generations of men? What could I do in four Argentine months of national holidays and strikes? I did what I could to teach the love of that literature, and I refrained as much as possible from dates and names.

Some female students came to see me. They had taken the

exam and passed. (All students pass with me!) To the girls—there were nine or ten—I said: "I have an idea. Now that you have passed and I have fulfilled my obligation as a professor, wouldn't it be interesting to embark on the study of a language or a literature we hardly know?" They asked which language and which literature. "Well, naturally the English language and English literature. Let us begin to study them, now that we are free from the frivolity of the exams; let us begin at the beginning."

I remembered that at home there were two books I could retrieve. I had placed them on the highest shelf, thinking I would never use them. They were Sweet's *Anglo-Saxon Reader* and *The Anglo-Saxon Chronicle*. Both had glossaries. And so we gathered one morning in the National Library.

I thought: I have lost the visible world, but now I am going to recover another, the world of my distant ancestors, those tribes of men who rowed across the stormy northern seas, from Germany, Denmark, and the Low Countries, who conquered England, and after whom we name England—since *Angle-land*, land of the Angles, had previously been called the land of the Britons, who were Celts.

It was a Saturday morning. We gathered in Groussac's office, and we began to read. It was a situation that pleased and mortified us, and at the same time filled us with a certain pride. It was the fact that the Saxons, like the Scandinavians, used two runic letters to signify the two sounds of *th,* as in *thing* and *the*. This conferred an air of mystery to the page.

We were encountering a language which seemed different from English but similar to German. What always happens, when one studies a language, happened. Each one of the words stood out as though it had been carved, as though it were a talisman. For that reason the poems of a foreign language have a prestige they do not enjoy in their own language, for one hears, one sees, each one of the words individually. We think of the beauty, of the power, or simply of the strangeness of them.

We had good luck that morning. We discovered the sentence, "Julius Caesar was the first Roman to discover England." Finding ourselves with the Romans in a text of the North, we were moved. You must remember we knew nothing of the language; each word was a kind of talisman we unearthed. We found two words. And with those two words we became almost drunk. (It's true that I was an old man and they were young women—likely stages for inebriation.) I thought: "I am returning to the language my ancestors spoke fifty generations ago; I am returning to that language; I am reclaiming it. It is not the first time I speak it; when I had other names this was the language I spoke." Those two words were the name of London, *Lundenburh,* and the name of Rome, which moved us even more, thinking of the light that had fallen on those northern islands, *Romeburh.* I think we left crying, "*Lundenburh, Romeburh* . . ." in the streets.

Thus I began my study of Anglo-Saxon, which blindness brought me. And now I have a memory full of poetry that is elegiac, epic, Anglo-Saxon.

I had replaced the visible world with the aural world of the Anglo-Saxon language. Later I moved on to the richer world of Scandinavian literature: I went on to the Eddas and the sagas. I wrote *Ancient Germanic Literature* and many poems based on those themes, but most of all I enjoyed it. I am now preparing a book on Scandinavian literature.

I did not allow blindness to intimidate me. And besides, my editor made me an excellent offer: he told me that if I produced thirty poems in a year, he would publish a book. Thirty poems means discipline, especially when one must dictate every line, but at the same time it allows for a sufficient freedom, as it is impossible that in one year there will not be thirty occasions for poetry. Blindness has not been for me a total misfortune; it should not be seen in a pathetic way. It should be seen as a way of life: one of the styles of living.

Being blind has its advantages. I owe to the darkness some gifts: the gift of Anglo-Saxon, my limited knowledge of Icelandic, the joy of so many lines of poetry, of so many poems, and of having written another book, entitled, with a certain falsehood, with a certain arrogance, *In Praise of Darkness.*

I would like to speak now of other cases, of illustrious cases. I will begin with that obvious example of the friendship of poetry and blindness, with one who has been called the greatest of poets: Homer. (We know of another blind Greek poet, Tamiris, whose work has been lost. Tamiris was defeated in a battle with the muses, who broke his lyre and took away his sight.)

Oscar Wilde had a curious hypothesis, one which I don't think is historically correct but which is intellectually agreeable. In general, writers try to make what they say seem profound; Wilde was a profound man who tried to seem frivolous. He wanted us to think of him as a conversationalist; he wanted us to consider him as Plato considered poetry, as "that winged, fickle, sacred thing." Well, that winged, fickle, sacred thing called Oscar Wilde said that Antiquity had deliberately represented Homer as blind.

We do not know if Homer existed. The fact that seven cities vie for his name is enough to make us doubt his historicity. Perhaps there was no single Homer; perhaps there were many Greeks whom we conceal under the name of Homer. The traditions are unanimous in showing us a blind poet, yet Homer's poetry is visual, often splendidly visual—as was, to a far lesser degree, that of Oscar Wilde.

Wilde realized that his poetry was too visual, and he

wanted to cure himself of that defect. He wanted to make poetry that was aural, musical—let us say like the poetry of Tennyson, or of Verlaine, whom he loved and admired so. Wilde said that the Greeks claimed that Homer was blind in order to emphasize that poetry must be aural, not visual. From that comes the "*de la musique avant toute chose*" of Verlaine and the symbolism contemporary to Wilde.

We may believe that Homer never existed, but that the Greeks imagined him as blind in order to insist on the fact that poetry is, above all, music; that poetry is, above all, the lyre; that the visual can or cannot exist in a poet. I know of great visual poets and great poets who are not visual—intellectual poets, mental ones—there's no need to mention names.

Let us go on to the example of Milton. Milton's blindness was voluntary. He knew from the beginning that he was going to be a great poet. This has occurred to other poets: Coleridge and De Quincey, before they wrote a single line, knew that their destiny was literary. I too, if I may mention myself, have always known that my destiny was, above all, a literary destiny—that bad things and some good things would happen to me, but that, in the long run, all of it would be converted into words. Particularly the bad things, since happiness does not need to be transformed: happiness is its own end.

Let us return to Milton. He destroyed his sight writing pamphlets in support of the execution of the king by Parliament. Milton said that he lost his sight voluntarily, defending freedom; he spoke of that noble task and never complained of being blind. He sacrificed his sight, and then he remembered his first desire, that of being a poet. They have discovered at Cambridge University a manuscript in which the young Milton proposes various subjects for a long poem.

"I might perhaps leave something so written to after-times, as they should not willingly let it die," he declared. He listed some ten or fifteen subjects, not knowing that one of them would prove prophetic: the subject of Samson. He did not know that his fate would, in a way, be that of Samson; that Samson, who had prophesied Christ in the Old Testament, also prophesied Milton, and with greater accuracy. Once he knew himself to be permanently blind, he embarked on two historical works, *A Brief History of Muscovia* and *A History of England*, both of which remained unfinished. And then the long poem *Paradise Lost*. He sought a theme that would interest all men, not merely the English. That subject was Adam, our common father.

He spent a good part of his time alone, composing verses, and his memory had grown. He would hold forty or fifty hendecasyllables of blank verse in his memory and then dictate them to whoever came to visit. The whole poem was written in this way. He thought of the fate of Samson, so close to his own, for now Cromwell was dead and the hour of the Restoration had come. Milton was persecuted and could have been condemned to death for having supported the execution of the king. But when they brought Charles II—son of Charles I, "The Executed"—the list of those condemned to death, he put down his pen and said, not without nobility, "There is something in my right hand which will not allow me to sign a sentence of death." Milton was saved, and many others with him.

He then wrote *Samson Agonistes*. He wanted to create a Greek tragedy. The action takes place in a single day, Samson's last. Milton thought on the similarity of destinies, since he, like Samson, had been a strong man who was ultimately defeated. He was blind. And he wrote those verses which, according to Landor, he punctuated badly, but which in fact had to be "Eyeless, in Gaza, at the mill, with the slaves"—as if the misfortunes were accumulating on Samson.

103

Milton has a sonnet in which he speaks of his blindness. There is a line one can tell was written by a blind man. When he has to describe the world, he says, "In this dark world and wide." It is precisely the world of the blind when they are alone, walking with hands outstretched, searching for props. Here we have an example—much more important than mine—of a man who overcomes blindness and does his work: *Paradise Lost, Paradise Regained, Samson Agonistes,* his best sonnets, parts of *A History of England,* from the beginnings to the Norman Conquest. All of this was executed while he was blind, all of it had to be dictated to casual visitors.

The Boston aristocrat Prescott was helped by his wife. An accident, when he was a student at Harvard, had caused him to lose one eye and left him almost blind in the other. He decided that his life would be dedicated to literature. He studied, and learned, the literatures of England, France, Italy, and Spain. Imperial Spain offered him a world which was agreeable to his own rigid rejection of a democratic age. From an erudite he became a writer, and he dictated to his wife, who read to him, the histories of the conquest of Mexico and Peru, of the reign of the Catholic Kings and of Phillip II. It was a happy labor, almost impeccable, which took more than twenty years.

There are two examples which are closer to us. One I have already mentioned, Paul Groussac, who has been unjustly forgotten. People see him now as a French interloper in Argentina. It is said that his historical work has become dated, that today one makes use of greater documentation. But they forget that Groussac, like every writer, left two works: first, his subject, and second, the manner of its execution. Groussac revitalized Spanish prose. Alfonso Reyes, the greatest prose writer in Spanish in any era, once told me, "Groussac taught me how Spanish should be written." Groussac overcame his blindness and left some of the best pages in prose that have been written in our country. It will always please me to remember this.

Let us recall another example, one more famous than Groussac. In James Joyce we are also given a twofold work. We have those two vast and—why not say it?—unreadable novels, *Ulysses* and *Finnegans Wake*. But that is only half of his work (which also includes beautiful poems and the admirable *Portrait of an Artist as a Young Man*). The other half, and perhaps the most redeeming aspect (as they now say) is the fact that he took on the almost infinite English language. That language—which is statistically larger than all the others and offers so many possibilities for the writer, particularly in its concrete verbs—was not enough for him. Joyce, an Irishman, recalled that Dublin had been founded by Danish Vikings. He studied Norwegian—he wrote a letter to Ibsen in Norwegian—and then he studied Greek, Latin . . . He knew all the languages, and he wrote in a language invented by himself, difficult to understand but marked by a strange music. Joyce brought a new music to English. And he said, valorously (and mendaciously) that "of all the things that have happened to me, I think the least important was having been blind." Part of his vast work was executed in darkness: polishing the sentences in his memory, working at times for a whole day on a single phrase, and then writing it and correcting it. All in the midst of blindness or periods of blindness. In comparison, the impotence of Boileau, Swift, Kant, Ruskin, and George Moore was a melancholic instrument for the successful execution of their work; one might say the same of perversion, whose beneficiaries today have ensured that no one will ignore their names. Democritus of Abdera tore his eyes out in a garden so that the spectacle of reality would not distract him; Origen castrated himself.

I have enumerated enough examples. Some are so illustrious that I am ashamed to have spoken of my own personal case—except for the fact that people always hope for confessions and I have no reason to deny them mine. But, of course, it seems absurd to place my name next to those I have recalled.

I have said that blindness is a way of life, a way of life that is not entirely unfortunate. Let us recall those lines of the greatest Spanish poet, Fray Luis de León:

> *Vivir quiero conmigo,*
> *gozar quiero del bien que debo al cielo,*
> *a solas sin testigo,*
> *libre de amor, de celo,*
> *de odio, de esperanza, de recelo.*

[I want to live with myself, /I want to enjoy the good that I owe to heaven, /alone, without witnesses, /free of love, of jealousy, /of hate, of hope, of fear.]

Edgar Allan Poe knew this stanza by heart.

For me to live without hate is easy, for I have never felt hate. To live without love I think is impossible, happily impossible for each one of us. But the first part—"I want to live with myself, /I want to enjoy the good that I owe to heaven"—if we accept that in the good of heaven there can also be darkness, then who lives more with themselves? Who can explore themselves more? Who can know more of themselves? According to the Socratic phrase, who can know himself more than the blind man?

A writer lives. The task of being a poet is not completed at a fixed schedule. No one is a poet from eight to twelve and from two to six. Whoever is a poet is one always, and continually assaulted by poetry. I suppose a painter feels that colors and shapes are besieging him. Or a musician feels that the strange world of sounds—the strangest world of art—is always seeking him out, that there are melodies and dissonances looking for him. For the task of an artist, blindness is not a total misfortune. It may be an instrument. Fray Luis de León dedicated one of his most beautiful odes to Francisco Salinas, a blind musician.

A writer, or any man, must believe that whatever happens to him is an instrument; everything has been given for an end. This is even stronger in the case of the artist. Everything that happens, including humiliations, embarrassments, misfortunes, all has been given like clay, like material for one's art. One must accept it. For this reason I speak in a poem of the ancient food of heroes: humiliation, unhappiness, discord. Those things are given to us to transform, so that we may make from the miserable circumstances of our lives things that are eternal, or aspire to be so.

If a blind man thinks this way, he is saved. Blindness is a gift. I have exhausted you with the gifts it has given me. It gave me Anglo-Saxon, it gave me some Scandinavian, it gave me a knowledge of a Medieval literature I had ignored, it gave me the writing of various books, good or bad, but which justified the moment in which they were written. Moreover, blindness had made me feel surrounded by the kindness of others. People always feel good will toward the blind.

I want to end with a line of Goethe: "*Alles Nahe werde fern,*" everything near becomes distant. Goethe was referring to the evening twilight. Everything near becomes distant. It is true. At nightfall, the things closest to us seem to move away from our eyes. So the visible world has moved away from my eyes, perhaps forever.

Goethe could be referring not only to twilight but to life.

All things go off, leaving us. Old age is probably the supreme solitude—except that the supreme solitude is death. And "everything near becomes distant" also refers to the slow process of blindness, of which I hoped to show, speaking tonight, that it is not a complete misfortune. It is one more instrument among the many—all of them so strange—that fate or chance provide.

Translated by Eliot Weinberger